I0822911

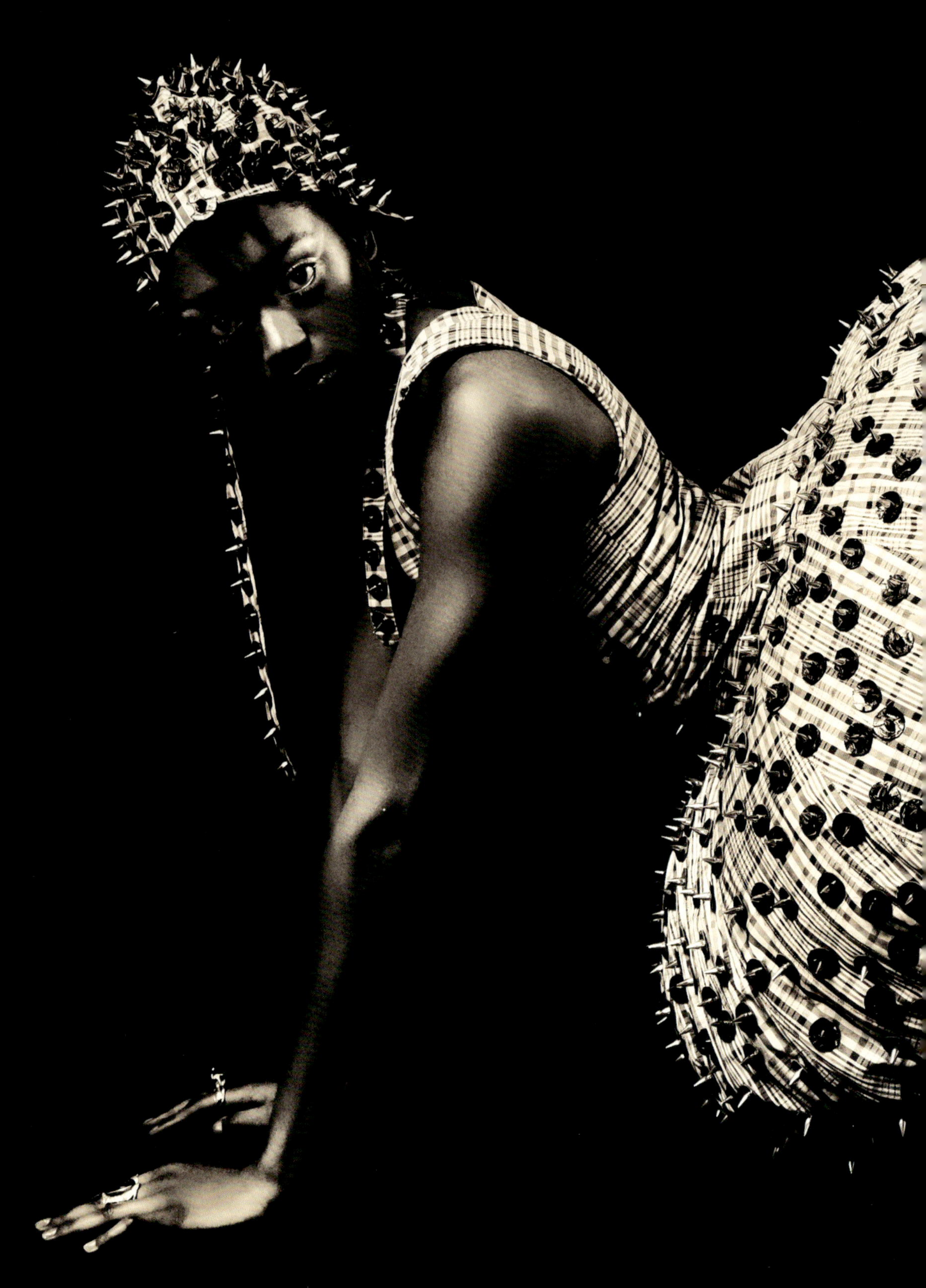

RAIHANNA

Shine

Portraits in Queer Resilience, Embracing New Dimensions

Asafe Ghalib

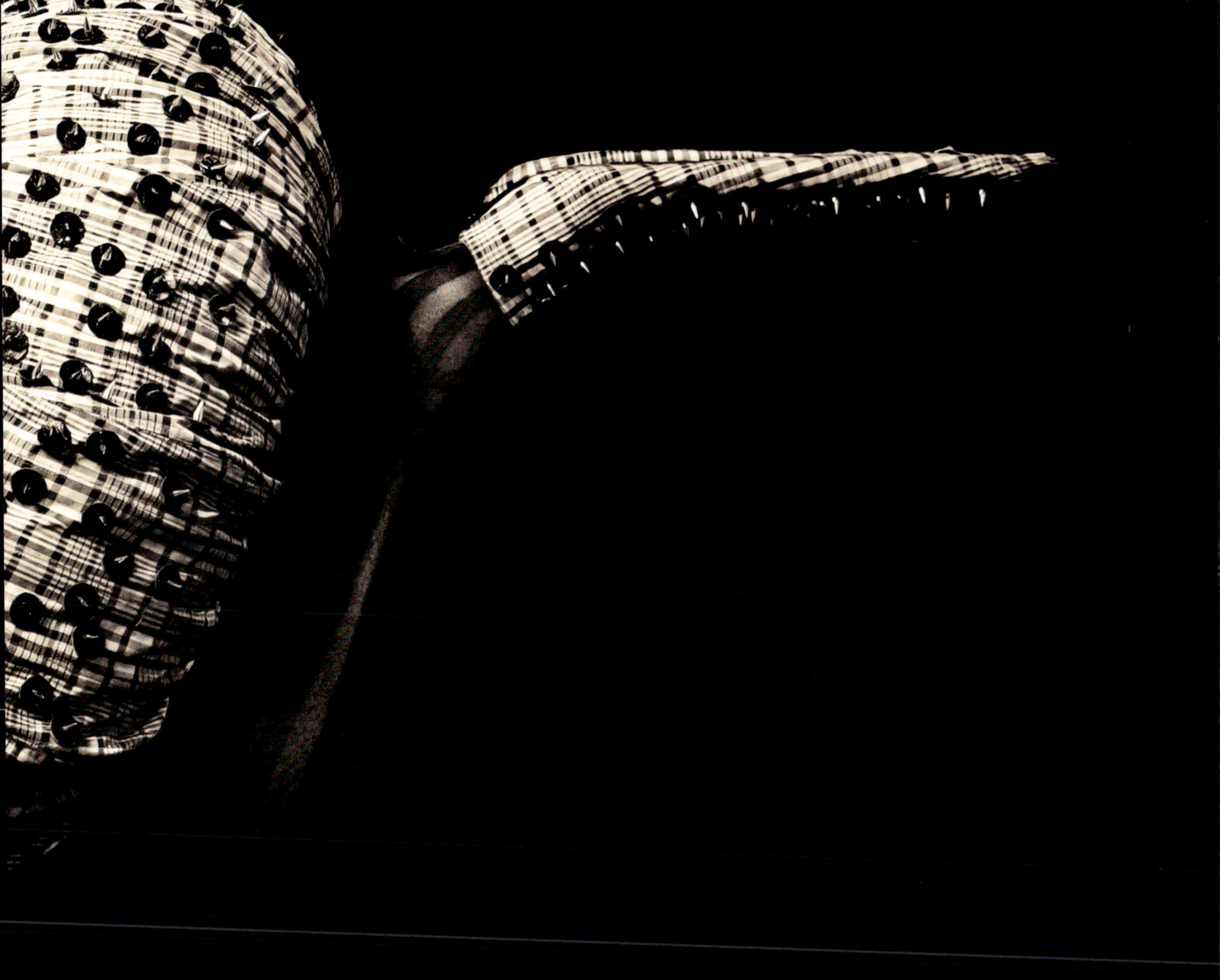

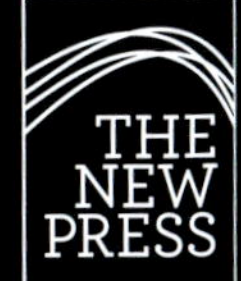

Published in the United States by The New Press, New York, 2025
Distributed by Two Rivers Distribution

ISBN 978-1-62097-977-8 (pb)
ISBN 979-8-89385-004-8 (ebook)
CIP data is available

The New Press publishes books that promote and enrich public discussion and understanding of the issues vital to our democracy and to a more equitable world. These books are made possible by the enthusiasm of our readers; the support of a committed group of donors, large and small; the collaboration of our many partners in the independent media and the not-for-profit sector; booksellers, who often hand-sell New Press books; librarians; and above all by our authors.

www.thenewpress.org

Book design and composition © 2025 by Emerson, Wajdowicz Studios (EWS)
This book was set in FranklinGothic URW, Helvetica, Orator, Rama Gothic, Wingdings, and Zapf Dingbats
Front cover image: Ebun Sodipo by Asafe Ghalib

Printed in the United States of America

10 9 8 7 6 5 4 3 2 1

Preface

JON STRYKER

This photobook series project was born out of conversations that I had with Jurek Wajdowicz. He is an accomplished art photographer and frequent collaborator of mine, and I am a lover and collector of photography. I owe a great debt to Jurek, to his design partner, Lisa LaRochelle, and to Yoko Yoshida-Carrera for bringing this book series to life.

Both Jurek and I have been extremely active in social justice causes—I as an activist and philanthropist and he as a creative collaborator with some of the household names in social change. Together we set out with an ambitious goal to explore and illuminate the most intimate and personal dimensions of self, still too often treated as taboo: sexual orientation and gender identity and expression. These books continue to reveal the amazing multiplicity in these core aspects of our being, played out against a vast array of distinct and varied cultures and customs from around the world.

Photography is a powerful medium for communication that can transform our understanding and awareness of the world we live in. We believe the photographs in this series will forever alter our perceptions of the arbitrary boundaries that we draw between others and ourselves and, at the same time, delight us with the broad spectrum of possibility for how we live our lives and love one another.

We are honored to have Asafe Ghalib as a collaborator in *Shine*. They and the other photographers in this ongoing series are more than craftspeople: they are communicators, translators, and facilitators of the kind of exchange that we hope will eventually allow all the world's people to live in greater harmony. ■

Jon Stryker, philanthropist, architect, and photography devotee, is the founder and board president of the Arcus Foundation, a global foundation promoting respect for diversity among peoples and in nature.

Introduction

PRISHITA MAHESHWARI-APLIN

For a people marginalized and erased, a photograph is much more than a 2-D snapshot of a moment in time. It's a form of protest, a bold claim to the fullness of our beings. It's also an archive, proof that we've always sought authentic expression in defiance of this suppression. And it's a route to creation, to innovation. The image acts as a conduit for an alternate reality, where one may be able to show up in ways this world rejects, stigmatizes, or makes unsafe. It allows us to exist within a transient state between the binary of conceptualization and realization; to occupy a space of *what could be* from *what is*. An image can tell stories of gender-bending fuckery, spotlight hidden diversity in a historical context, and transplant the demonized into scenes of normalcy. It can also both create fictionalized, yet honest, scenes of shared transgression and capture the raw truth in all its messy complexity.

Through these high-contrast intimate portraits, Asafe Ghalib builds on a long legacy of queer visual storytelling. Creative expression has always been deeply necessary for the LGBTQIA+ community—"a compulsion, a desire, to make their presence known."[1] Indeed, for much of humanity (much further back than a cis-heteronormative and colonial reading of art history), countless works ranging from sculptures adorning Hindu temples and homoerotic Athenian vase paintings, to Japanese woodblock prints and nineteenth-century French paintings that capture lesbian desire, have written queerness into a visual artistic canon. However, photography, in particular, offers something more tangible, more immediate. It brings the metaphorical and fantastical into the realms of reality. Through the art of documentary—whether manufactured or not—it more directly confronts the hegemonic forces that seek to keep us *contained/containable* and *categorized/categorizable*.

Thus, something transformational takes place in the coded space held between the image and us as the audience. A portal appears with pulsating edges, an alternate dimension of innovation. A world within that reflects society back onto itself, yet exposes, distorts, or upsets the status quo to create room for something different, better, or simply more meaningful. A liminal space, laden with interpretation, which creates understanding and acceptance of our deviance. A heterotopia, which models a fairer universe, distinct from or directly subverting oppressive expectations in society.[2] Here, the queer "alien"—the terrible, the "ugly," the perverse—is celebrated. The "othered" is brought into sharp focus, centered in a narrative shaped by their own vulnerable gaze. The camp sensibility is able to revel in its multiplicity as a reclamation of the "too much."

In *Shine*, Asafe celebrates this queer culture of "camp" through representations of their friends and community members. These figures, draped in structured silhouettes and lit by dramatic light and shadow, serve to bastardize the expected. Figures of all shapes and sizes dazzle in various states of *dress/undress/overdress*, with top surgery scars a *meaningful/meaningless* reality and faces painted with a heavy but artful hand. While Black and Brown queers, fat beings and butch dykes embrace through exaggeration and defiance their terribleness—their "ugliness" in the eyes of white supremacy and the patriarchy—to disrupt conventional ideals of beauty and femininity. The enclosed images expertly highlight gender as "constructed identity, a performative accomplishment," as posited by gender studies scholar Judith Butler in 1988[3] by adopting a camp lens that perceives Beings-as-Playing-a-Role in "the metaphor of life as theatre."[4] And, in doing so, they encourage us to reflect on, understand, and question the role we play in delivering these often harmful prewritten scripts. The fact that some may perceive aspects of these portraits as "ridiculous" only serves to clarify what is, in fact, ridiculous—the lengths taken to uphold the fabricated idea of a binary and dimorphic "normal."

The identities of "monster" and "alien" being thrust upon the marginalized as insult and subsequently reclaimed by the proud deviant has long held meaning for the queer community. Indeed, heterotopic universes home to such characters crafted by science fiction, fantasy, and horror genres allow trans+ individuals in particular to represent and explore otherness, body modification, self-creation, power, and alternative governance structures. Meanwhile, the term "alien," which has been official terminology describing noncitizens in U.S. legislation since the late 1700s, is now recognized as dehumanizing language that stigmatizes migrants and refugees, and contributes to a hostile environment for those who take the brave step to cross oceans and borders to rebuild lives. This has become all too apparent in the free usage of the label "illegal alien" by President Donald Trump, who has since invoked the eighteenth-century Alien and Sedition Acts to bolster racist and violent powers of the U.S. Immigration and Customs Enforcement (ICE).

Both queerphobia and anti-immigrant sentiment are driven by a capitalist scarcity myth, propagated via the scapegoating of marginalized groups by a power-hungry minority. Through feeding on a fear of the unknown, national pride rooted in a need for belonging, and a conservative drive to preserve the status quo, these bad actors are able to sustain such narratives, especially during and following times of economic instability and crisis. Within this context, Ghalib's ongoing *Queer Immigrants* series holds immense power to cast light on the shared roots of and parallels between our struggles, and thus the shared pathways to our collective liberation. The queer immigrant, outsider two times over, may be "othered" in more than one space—questioned or rejected for multiple facets of their intersectional identity. While this can create an unmooredness, an untethered sense of self, it can also offer us the chance to carve out new pathways—or indeed new dimensions—in pursuit of authentic expression, connection, and community. →

As we decolonize the self, uncoupling notions of gender, beauty, and belonging from white supremacy, we also come to question other structures positioned to us as "normal." Chosen families—"families formed outside of biological or legal (bio-legal) bonds"[5]—and mutual aid networks have been life-saving and life-affirming for migrants and queers alike. They've sustained communities, such as mixed-status immigrant Latinx families surviving the lack and loss of grandparents, aunts, brothers. They also have created longevity where there easily could've been none, such as for the terminally ill gay men living with HIV, and ostracized by their bio-legal families, who received end-of-life care from lesbians who usually "didn't want to have anything to do with men—even gay men."[6]

Something metamorphic takes place via the formation of such alternative kin dynamics. Within these heterotopias, we, who experience otherness in relation to the outside world, morph into authenticity via experiencing togetherness with one another. When we root our acts of care in this sometimes sacrificial love—solidarity that is often boundless and boundaryless—we are freed from prescriptive definitions of "family," "responsibility," and "love." Through these familial structures of our own creation, we practice what Simone de Beauvoir hypothesized as "authentic love." Although originally proposed in the context of heterosexual romantic relationships, it sits in contrast to "inauthentic love" as love that is nonpossessive and nonsubmissive. It both acknowledges our differences and considers us as equals in relationality. It's a love that not only recognizes, respects, and embodies our own erotic power, but holds up a mirror to the other to affirm and share in theirs, too.

When I speak of erotic power in this context, I build on the thinking of Black feminist writer and activist Audre Lorde, who framed the erotic not only as a sexual feeling or activity, but also as a "personification of love in all its aspects."[7] For Lorde, by forming a bridge between "those physical, emotional, and psychic expressions" of love in its deepest meanings, the erotic acts as one resource among "various sources of power within the culture of the oppressed that can provide energy for change." Asafe's creative decision to reference the traditional family portrait, partially through monochrome and sepia colorways, speaks to the chosen family as "a refuge specifically generated by and for the queer experience—a core cultural motif that spans generations and borders."[8] Thus, this work draws attention to the power held and created by both queer and migrant communities, and queer immigrants perhaps twofold, to channel this potential energy into driving real change for the individual and the collective.

We model the world we want to see and create within our interpersonal relationships, and the reimagination of family to center healing and reciprocity is one powerful route that we have toward liberated futures. The chosen family offers an alternative to the nuclear heteronormative family that promotes traditional gender roles and upholds capitalism by perpetuating inequality, contributing to compartmentalization of neighborhoods and communities. It also creates a queer time and space that exists "in opposition to the institutions of family, heterosexuality, and reproduction," as argued by Jack Halberstam in *In a Queer Time and Place*. Indeed, the family portrait also nods to the world-making qualities of queer temporality. In a literal sense, it implants queerness within a historical time and place, one where it may in reality have been persecuted. There also is a timelessness created by the stark and confronting poses, the nods to Victorian-era fashion, the jester trope, and much ethereal futurism, that draws invisible threads of connection between *then/now* and *what is/what could be*.

Through collaborative portrait making, Asafe not only creates a heterotopic ideal where the perspectives of the "othered" are centered, but also fosters collectivity. This speaks to the cumulative force for change that queer creativity can inspire when experienced as a shared eroticism that builds bridges between us. This togetherness is vital now as we face a rise in queer- and transphobia, an impending climate crisis, and the ongoing violence of colonial projects across the world. Ghalib's work spotlights the role that imaginative, intimate, and honest art can—and must—play in our defense against the rise of fascism. As Susan Sontag writes in her essay "Our Culture and the New Sensibility": "Art today is a new kind of instrument for modifying consciousness and organizing new modes of sensibility."[9] We cannot, and must not, separate art from the context within which it is borne. Art is inherently political and I truly believe that work like this has the power to bring us closer to one another—to turn toward one another and accept the fullness of our fears and our flaws—not to excuse harm, but rather to find new routes to understanding, rehabilitation, and liberated futures. ■

1 Castle, T. in *The Female Closet* (1998). Directed by Barbara Hammer. US: Barbara Hammer.
2 Foucault, M. (1984). "Of Other Spaces: Utopias and Heterotopias," *Architecture /Mouvement/ Continuité,* no. 5, pp. 46–49.
3 Butler, J. (1988). "Performative Acts and Gender Constitution: An Essay in Phenomenology and Feminist Theory," *Theatre Journal*, 40(4), pp. 519–531.
4 Sontag, S. (1966). "Notes on Camp," in Sontag, S. *Against Interpretation and Other Essays*. NY: Dell.
5 Levin, N. J. et al. (2020). "'We Just Take Care of Each Other': Navigating 'Chosen Family' in the Context of Health, Illness, and the Mutual Provision of Care amongst Queer and Transgender Young Adults," *International Journal of Environmental Research and Public Health,* 17(19). doi:10.3390/ijerph17197346.
6 Women's Museum of California (2019). *The Blood Sisters of San Diego.* Available at: https://womensmuseum.wordpress. com/2019/04/10/the-blood-sisters-of-san-diego/.
7 Lorde, A. (1984). "Uses of the Erotic: The Erotic as Power," in Lorde, A. *Sister Outsider: Essays and Speeches*. CA: The Crossing Press, pp. 53–55.
8 Weston, K. (1997). *Families We Choose: Lesbians, Gays, Kinship*. Revised edition. NY: Columbia University Press.
9 Sontag, S. (1966). "Our Culture and the New Sensibility," in Sontag, S. *Against Interpretation*.

Queer Immigrants

My work aims to capture people within a historical context in order to bring awareness to the long-resisting and historically misrepresented Queer community. The Queer community has taught me to express myself without boundaries and it is where I found a sense of freedom and belonging. It is important to me that my work provokes, informs, and creates a safe space for the viewer through the exploration of identity. Consisting of mostly black-and-white and sepia photography, the use of monochromatic colors resembles a newspaper and historical photographs from old books and magazines as well as traditional family photos, a type of portraiture that has been present since the invention of photography. It is by embracing these parameters that I create a place to be reclaimed, showing the importance of each and every person that I photograph in their own manner.

My focus is to photograph individuals that are part of the LGBTQIA+ community, including friends and fellow artists. I mostly photograph individuals by themselves in order to allow their personality to emerge in full bloom. The space we create together during the photo shoot is a special occasion where we can learn from each other and communicate the person's ideas in their rawest, most beautiful, and most empowered form. My work is an act of both confrontation and pride. It is a collective effort to reshape the narrative surrounding our community and challenge the misconceptions that have perpetuated our misrepresentation. Through visual storytelling, I invite viewers to embark on this journey with us, immersing themselves in the complexities and triumphs of our lives. By sharing our stories and experiences, I aim to confront societal expectations and stereotypes, ultimately fostering a more accurate understanding of our community's identity. Through collaboration, my work becomes a powerful platform for the Queer community to reclaim agency, inspiring others to question the status quo, and promoting positive change within our society.

—ASAFE

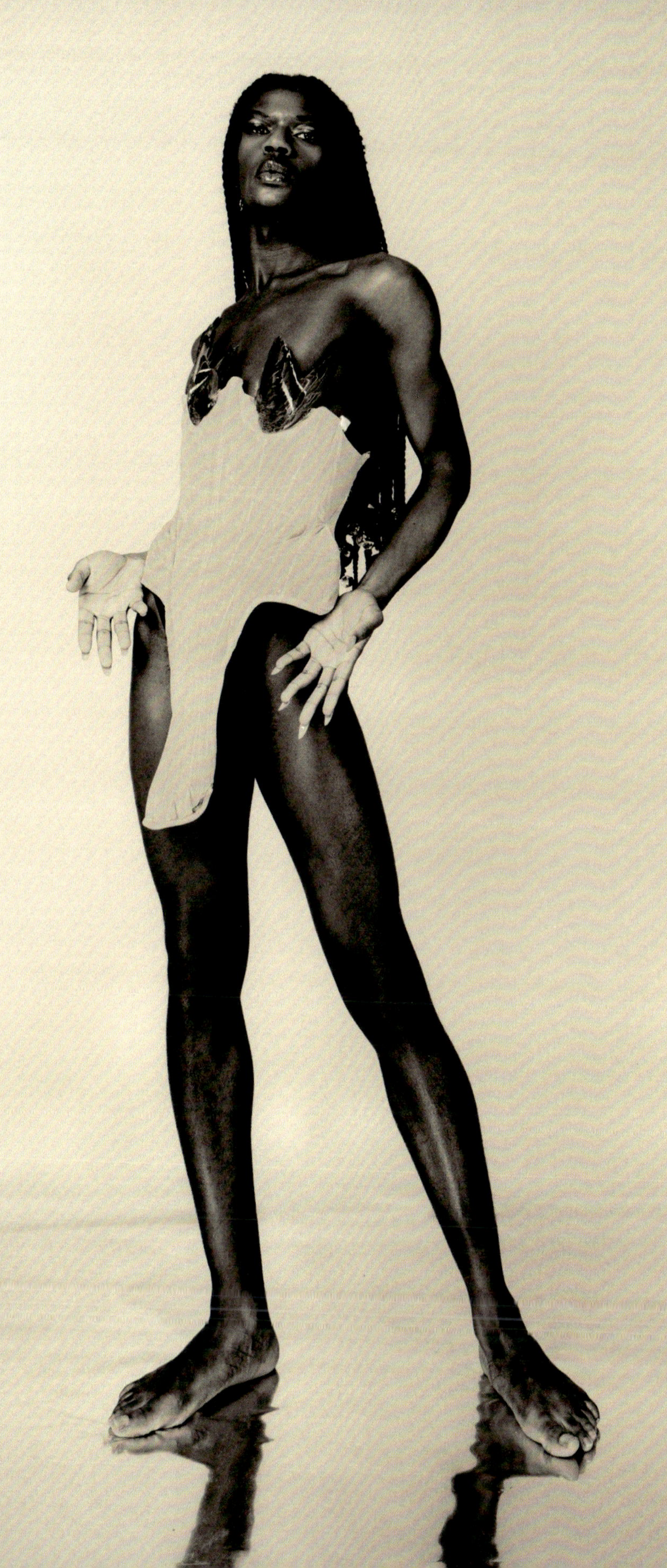

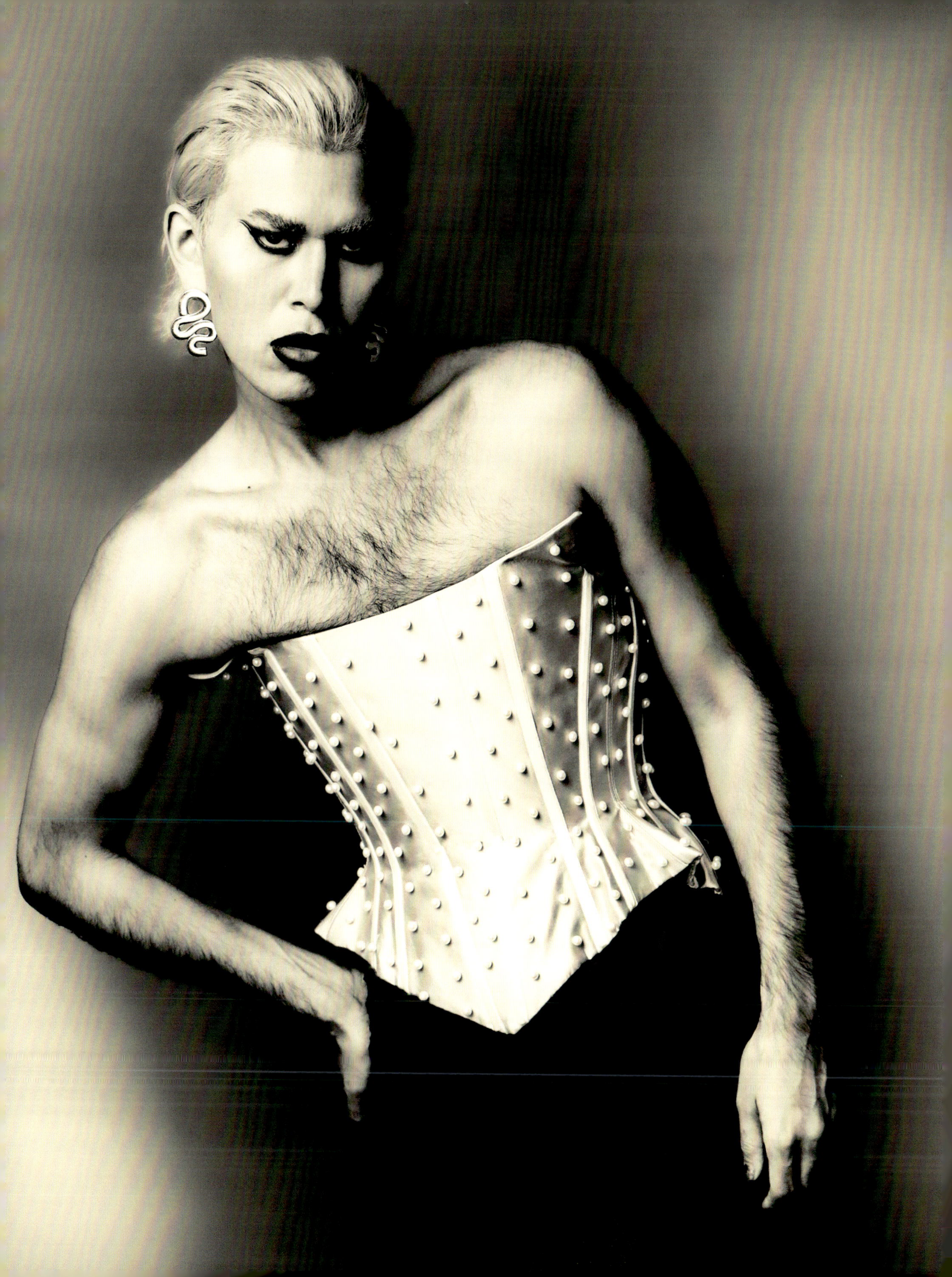

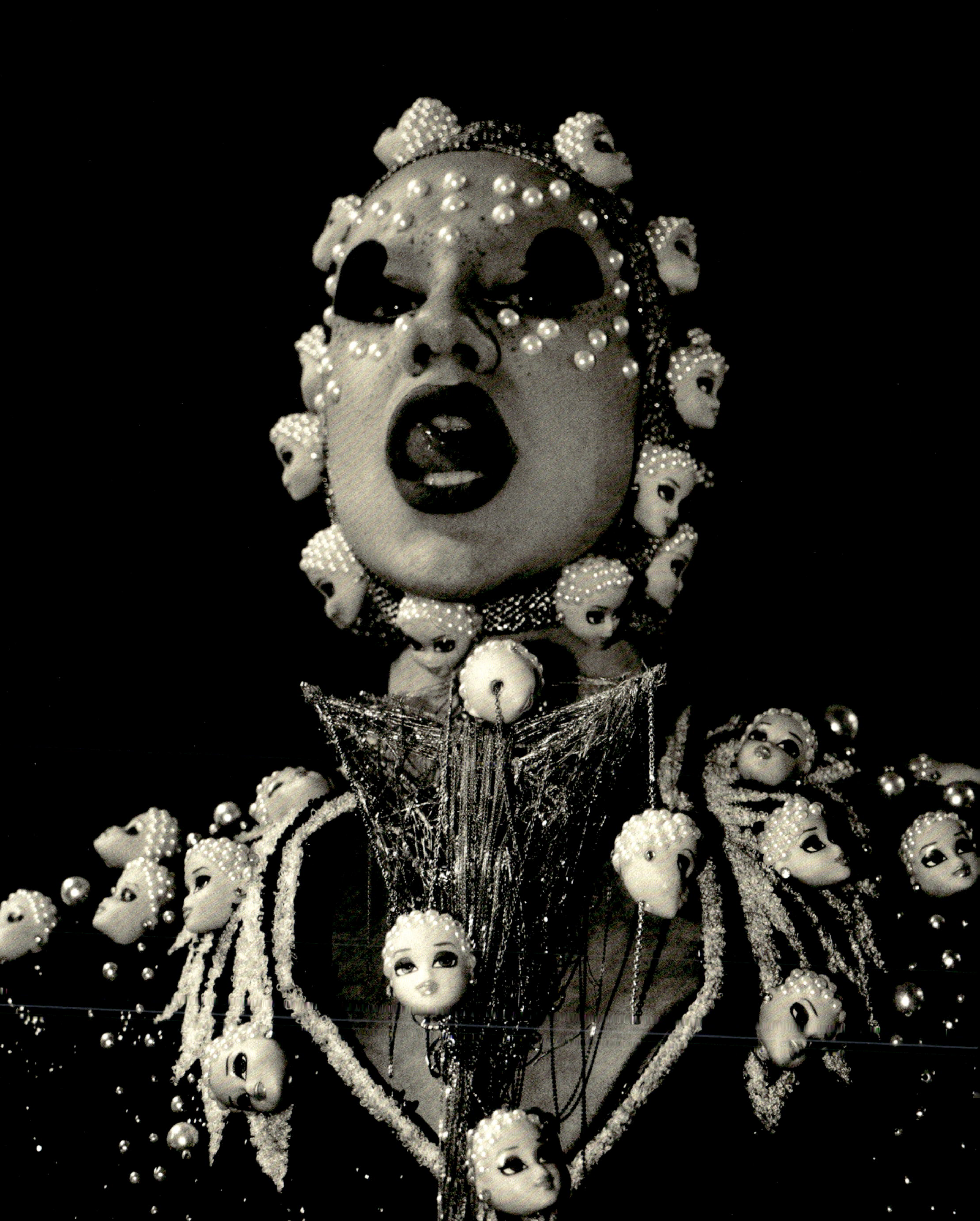

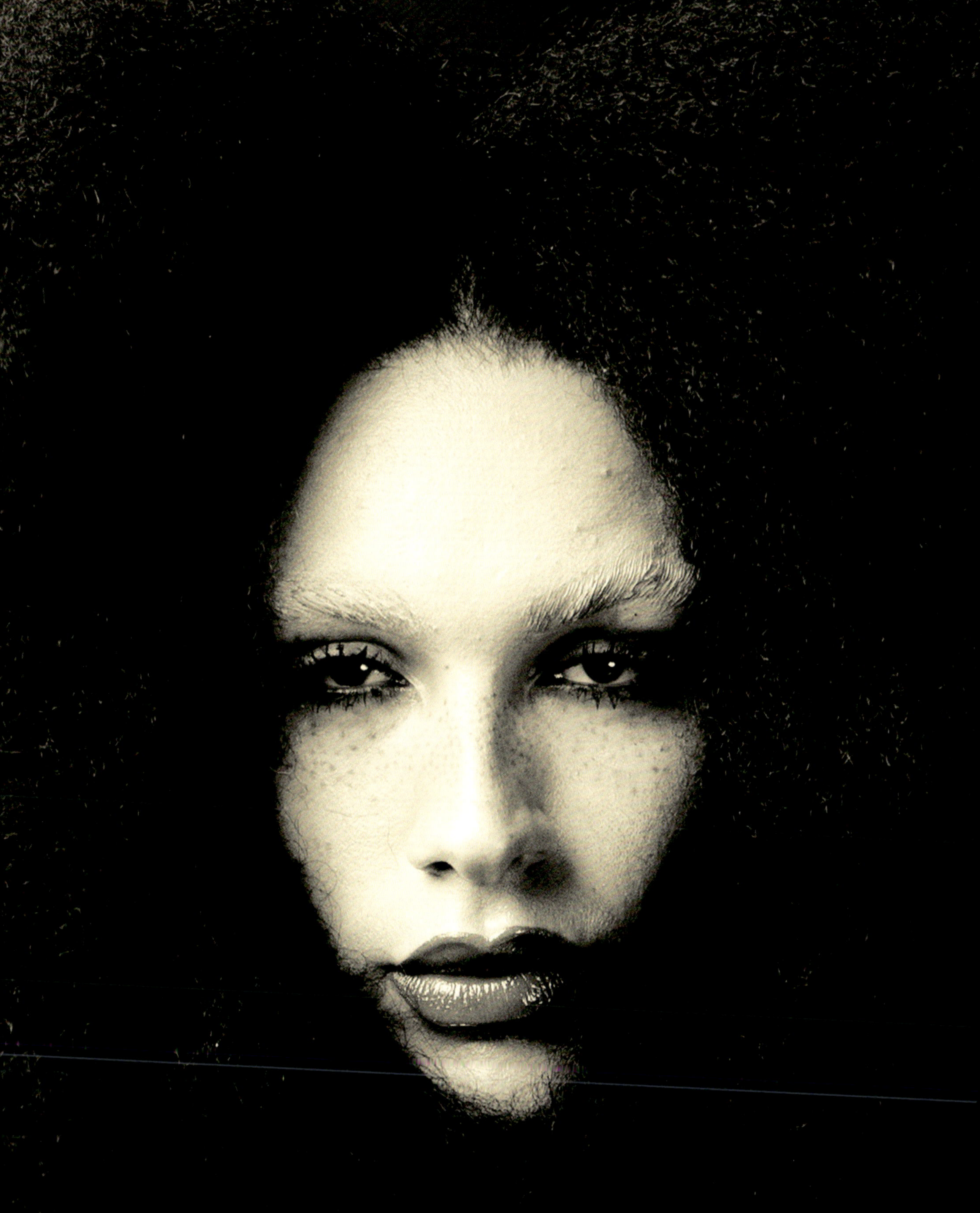

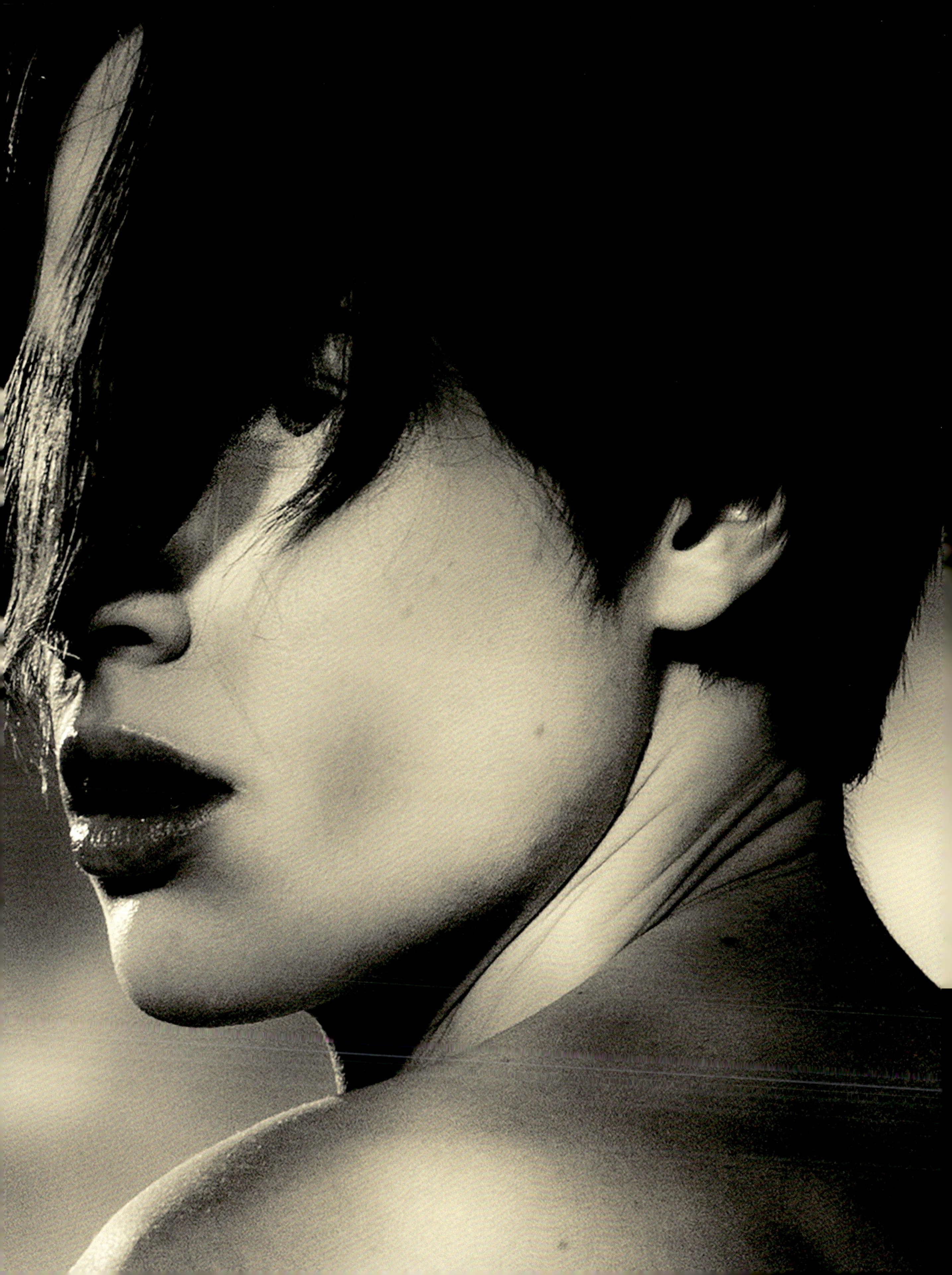

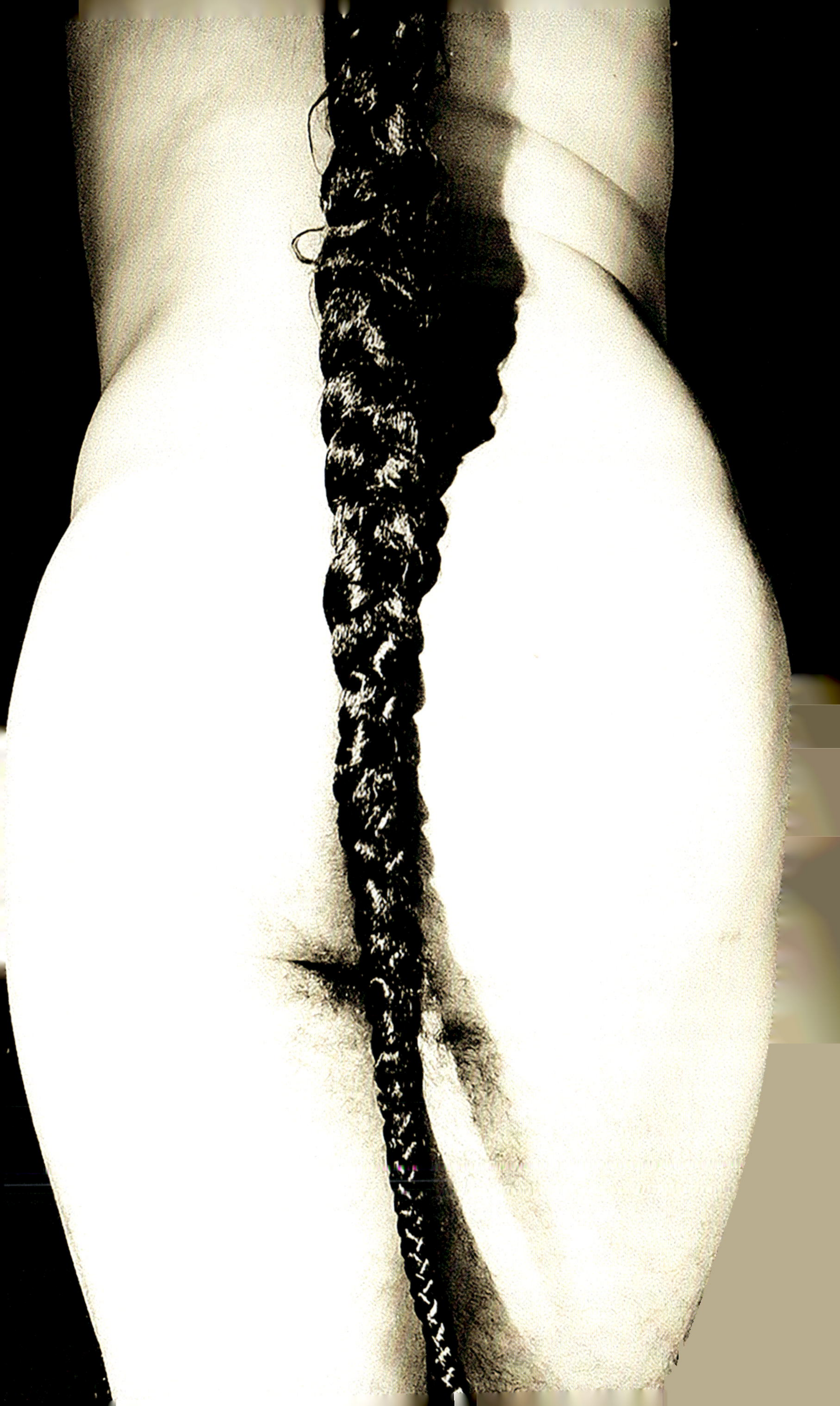

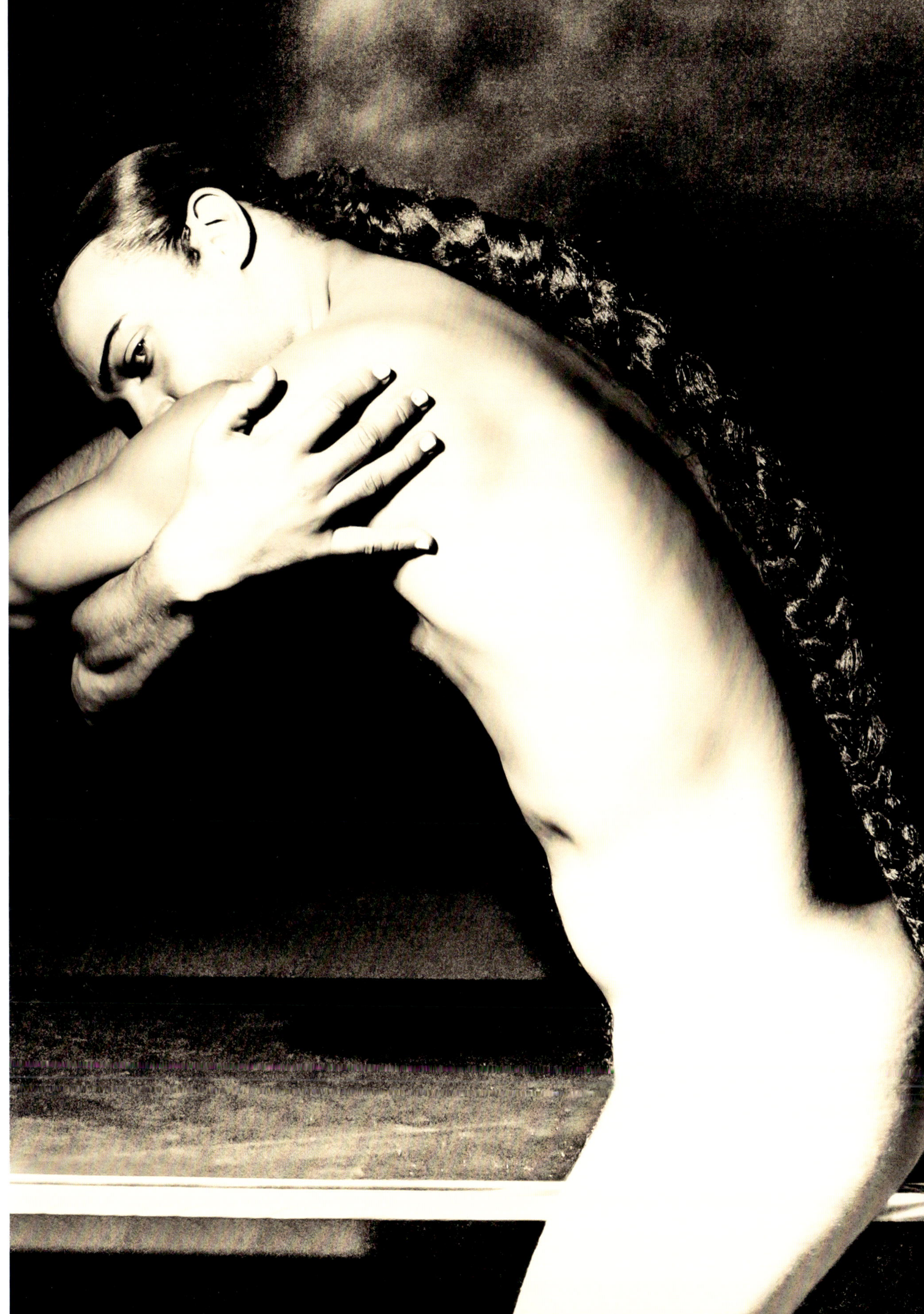

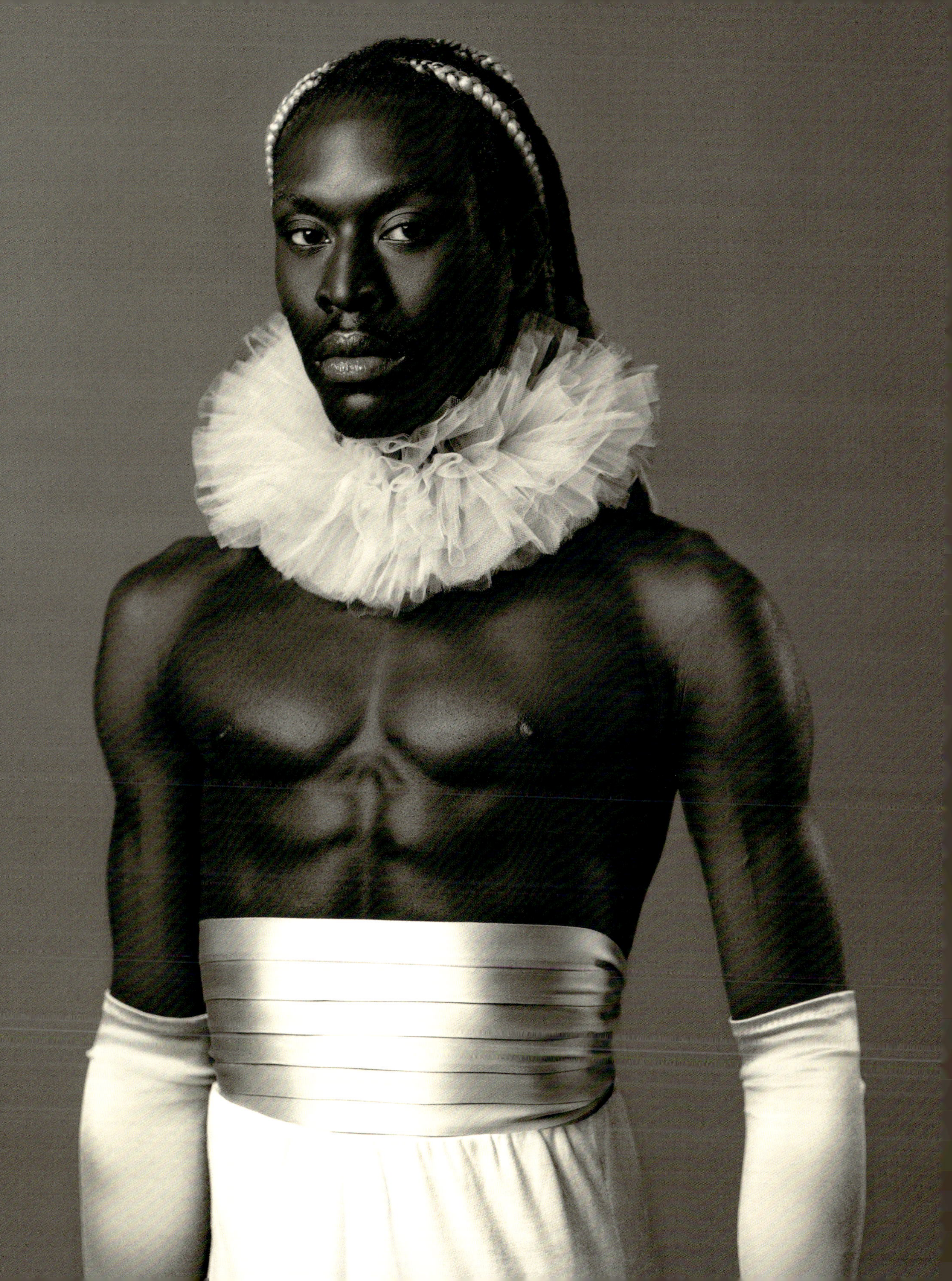

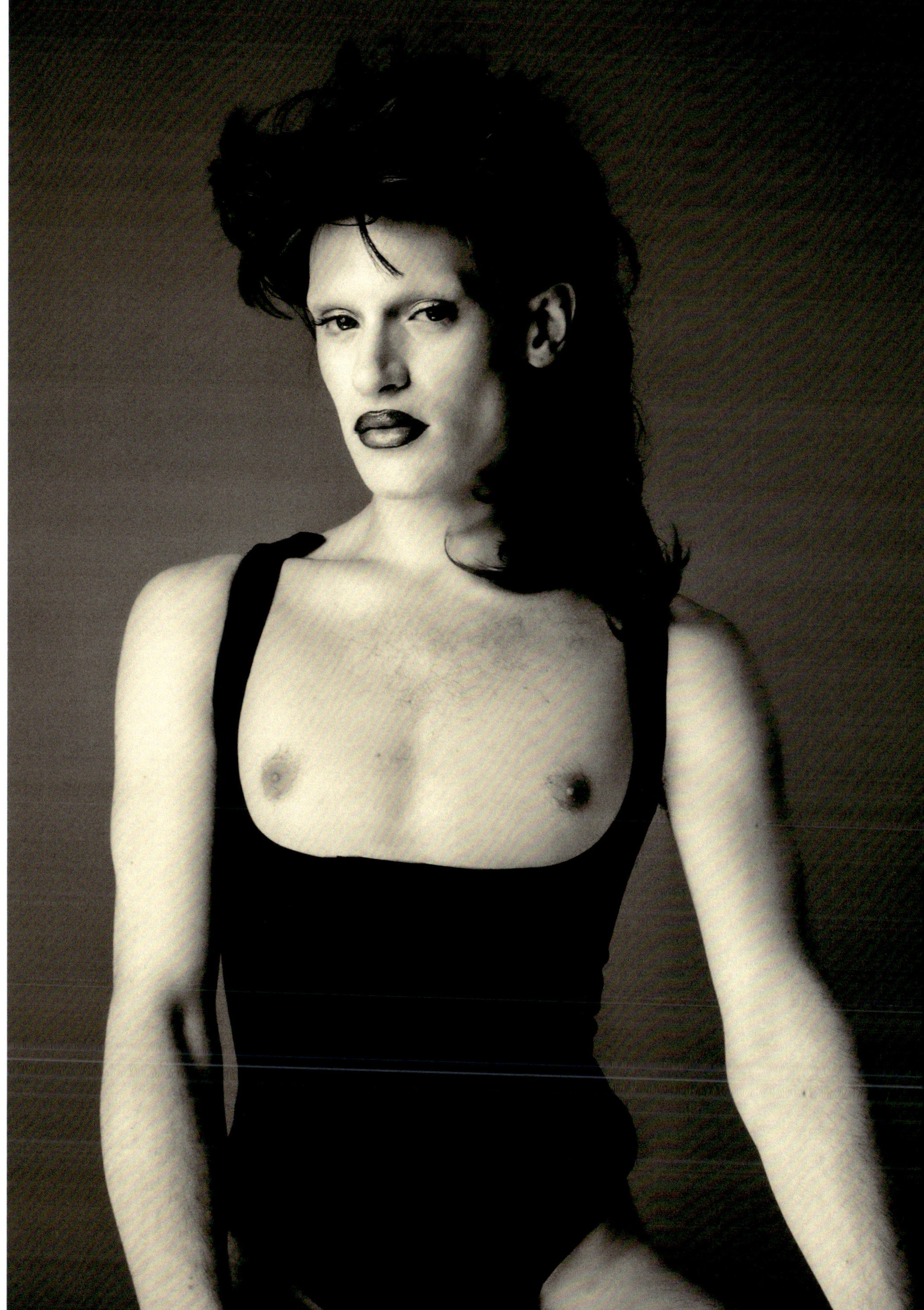

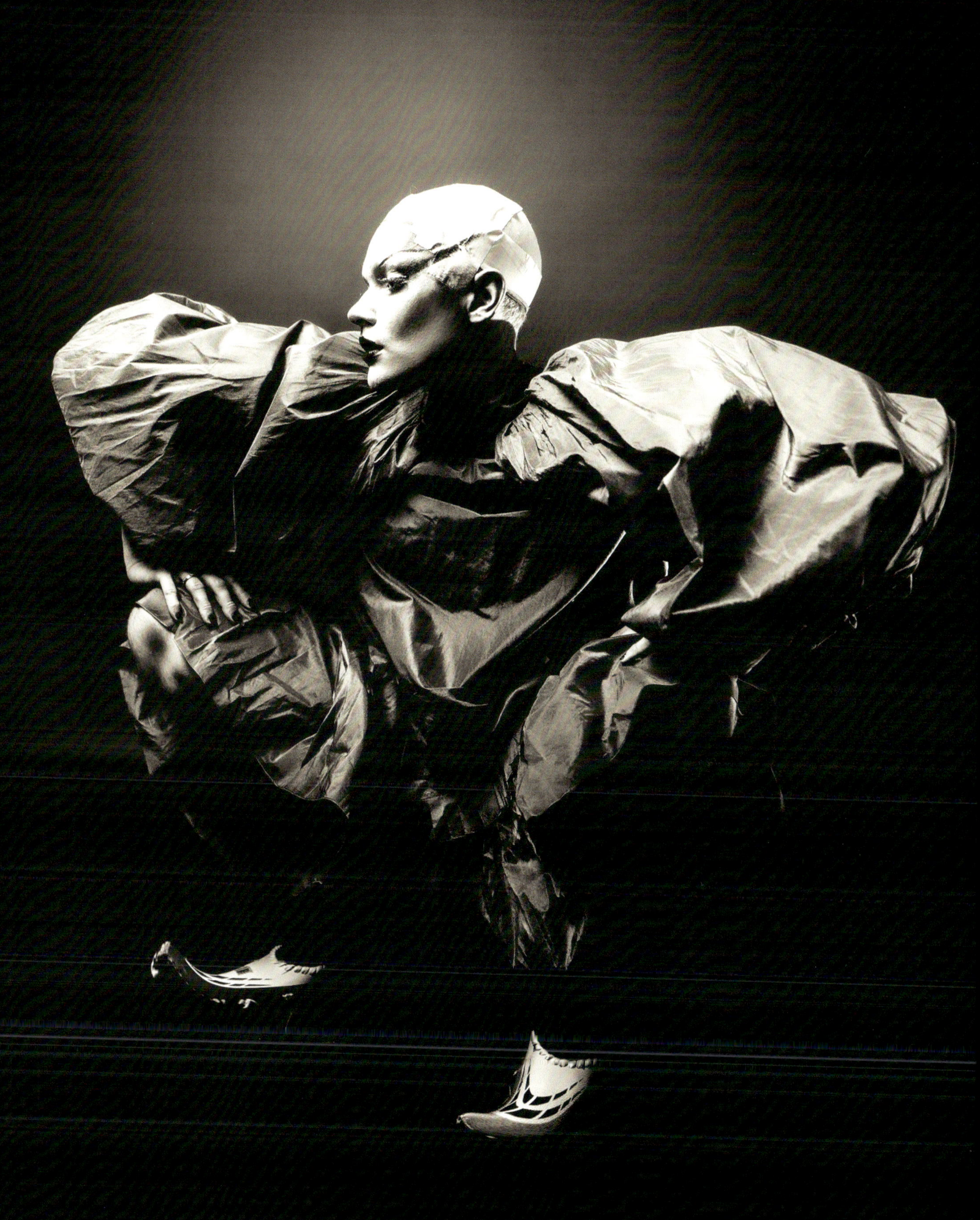

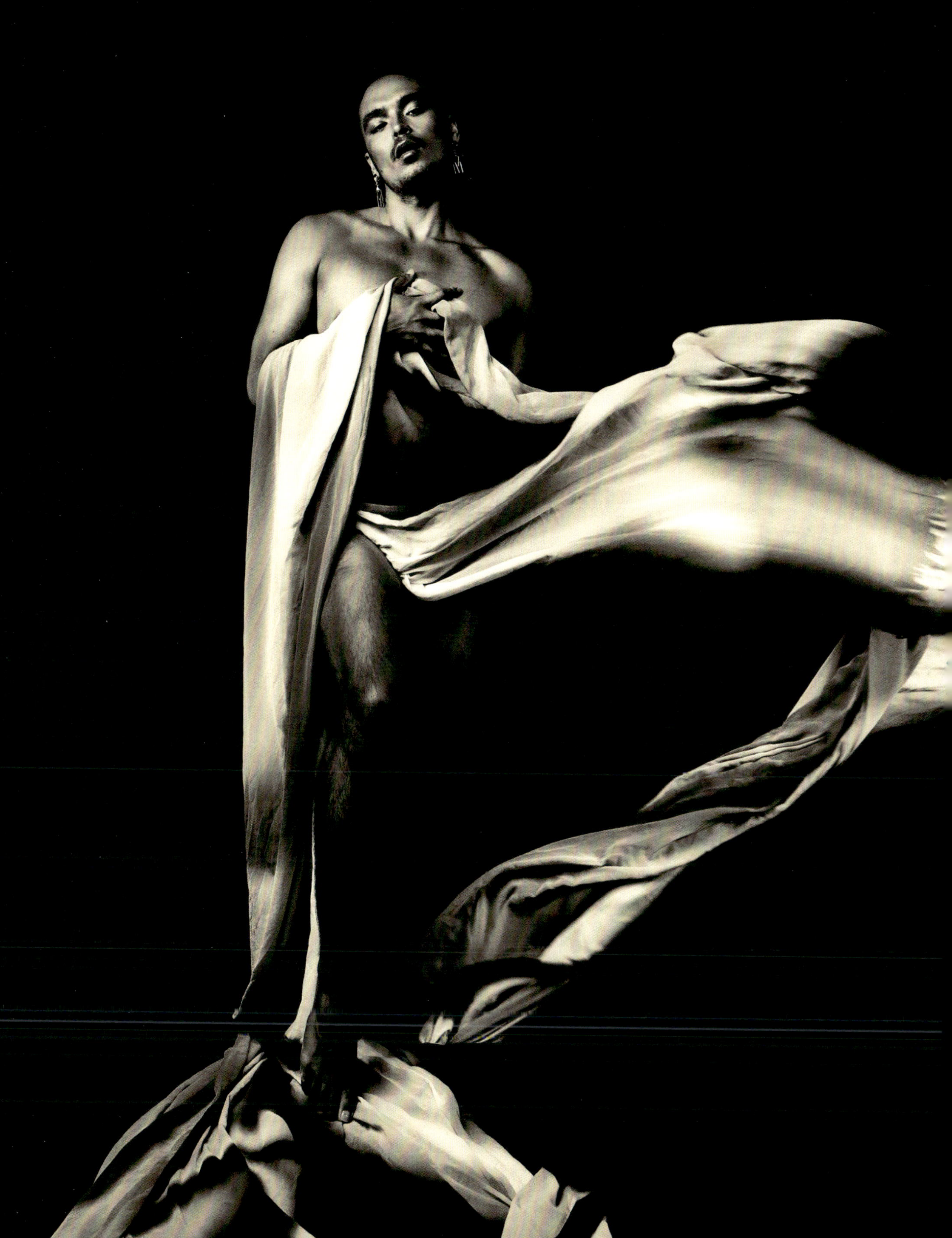

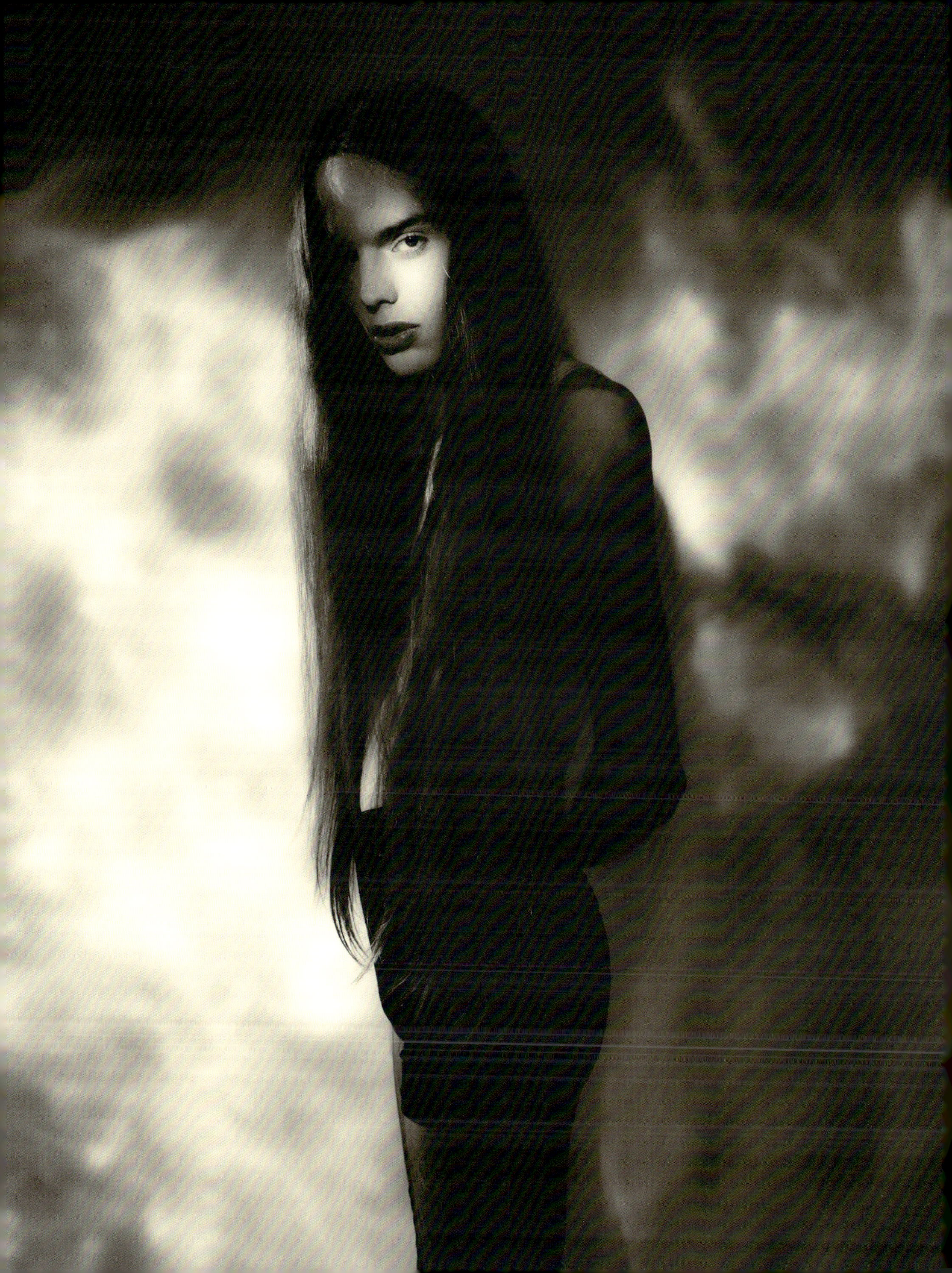

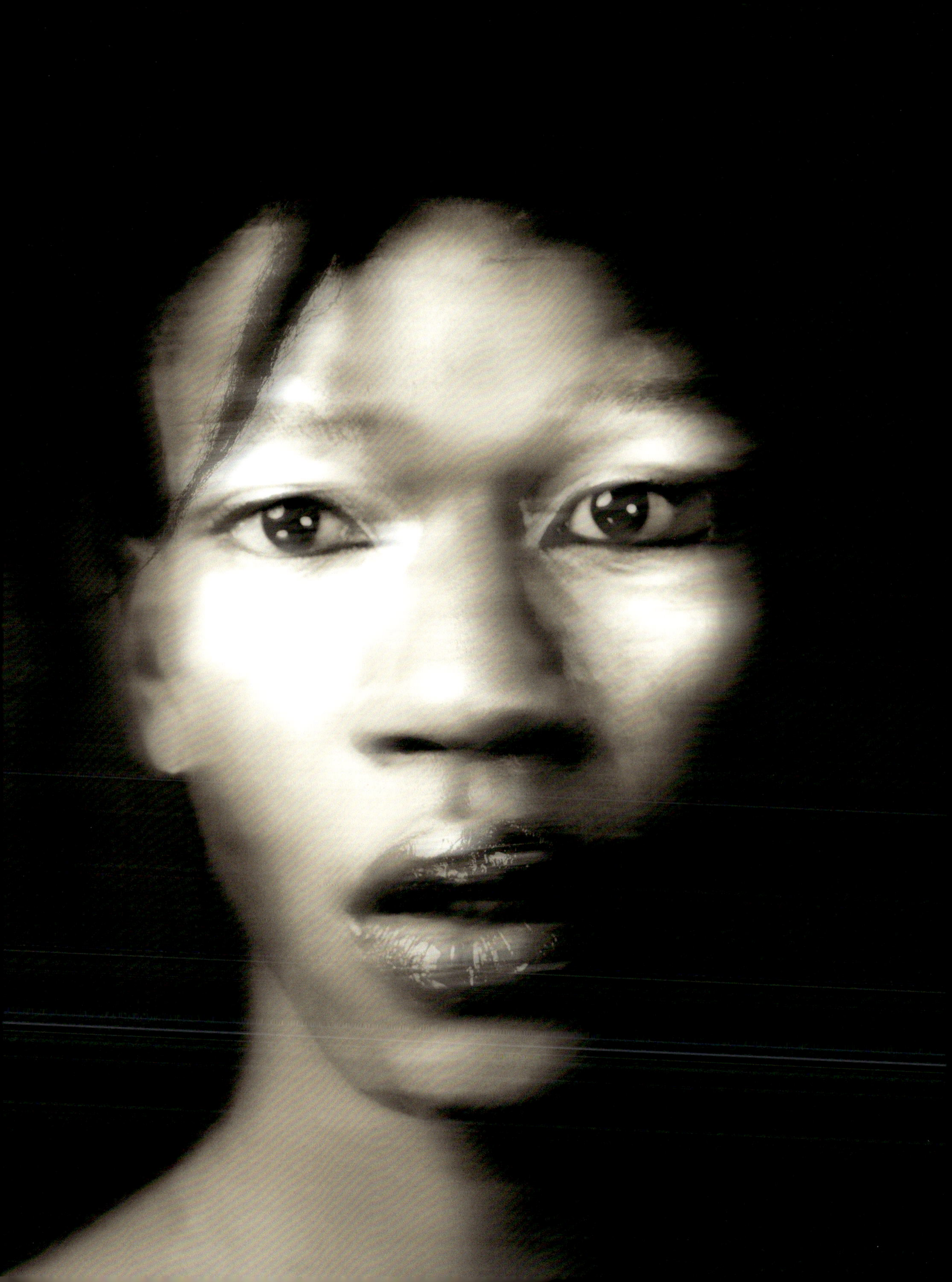

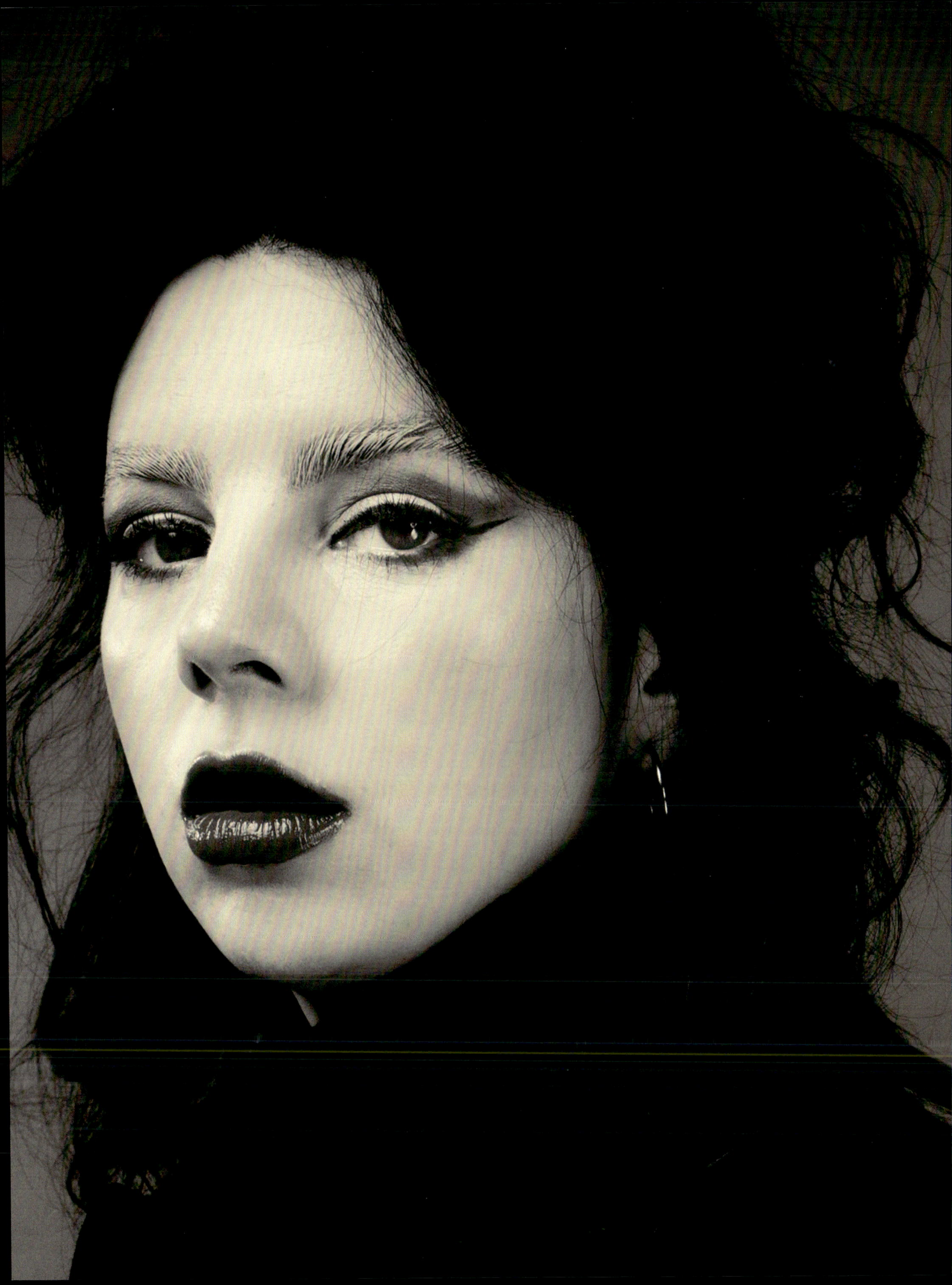

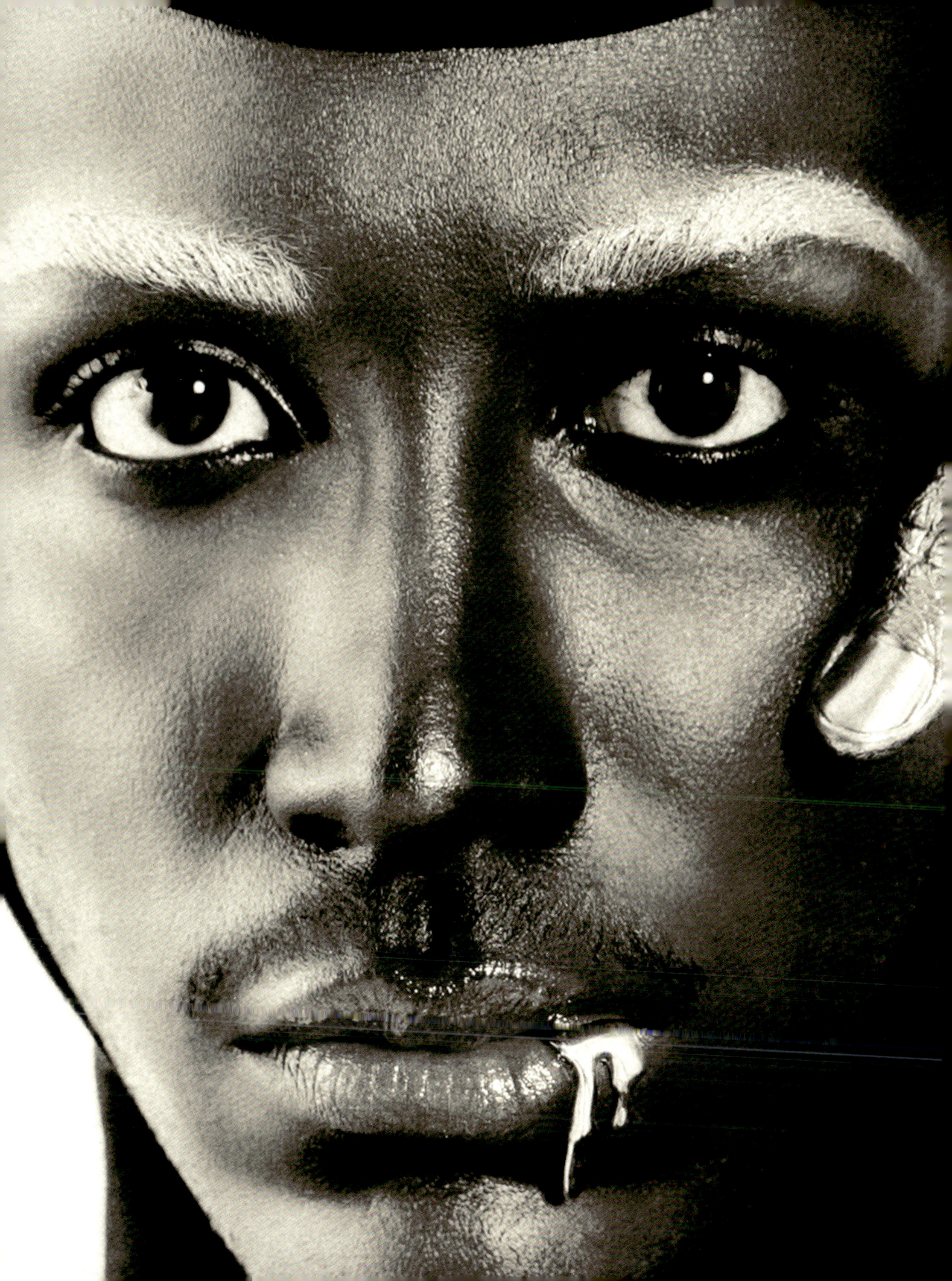

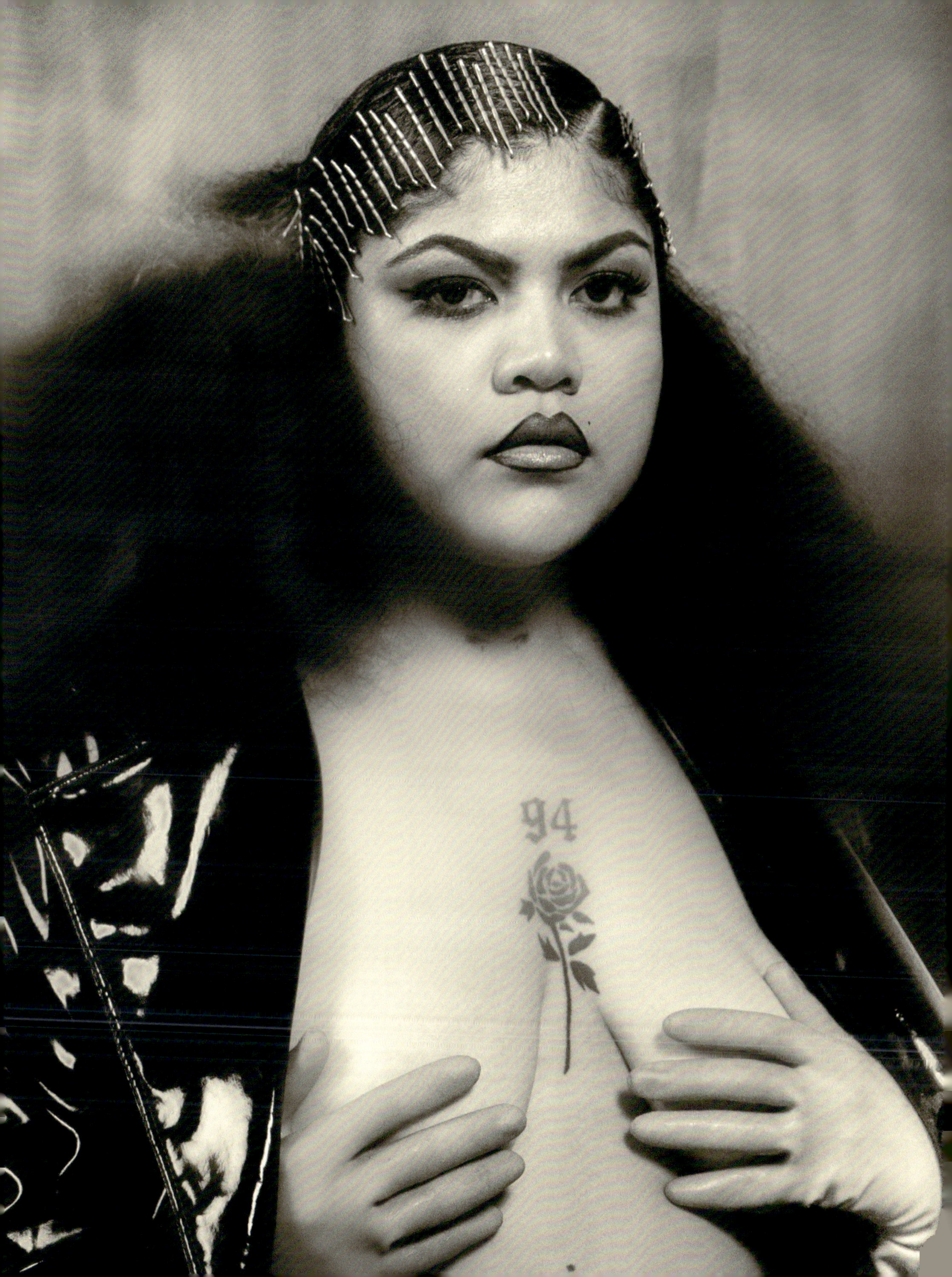
94

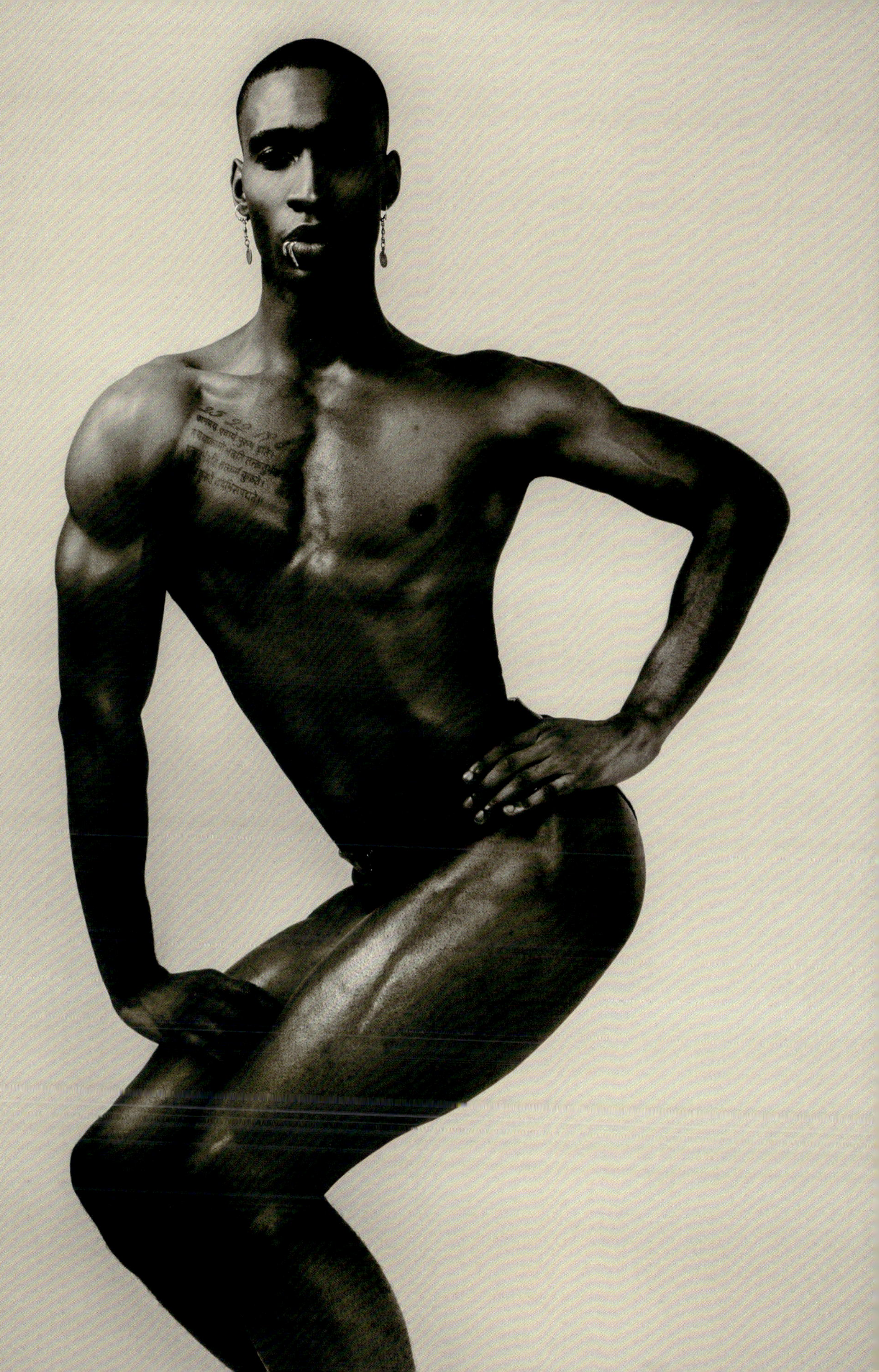

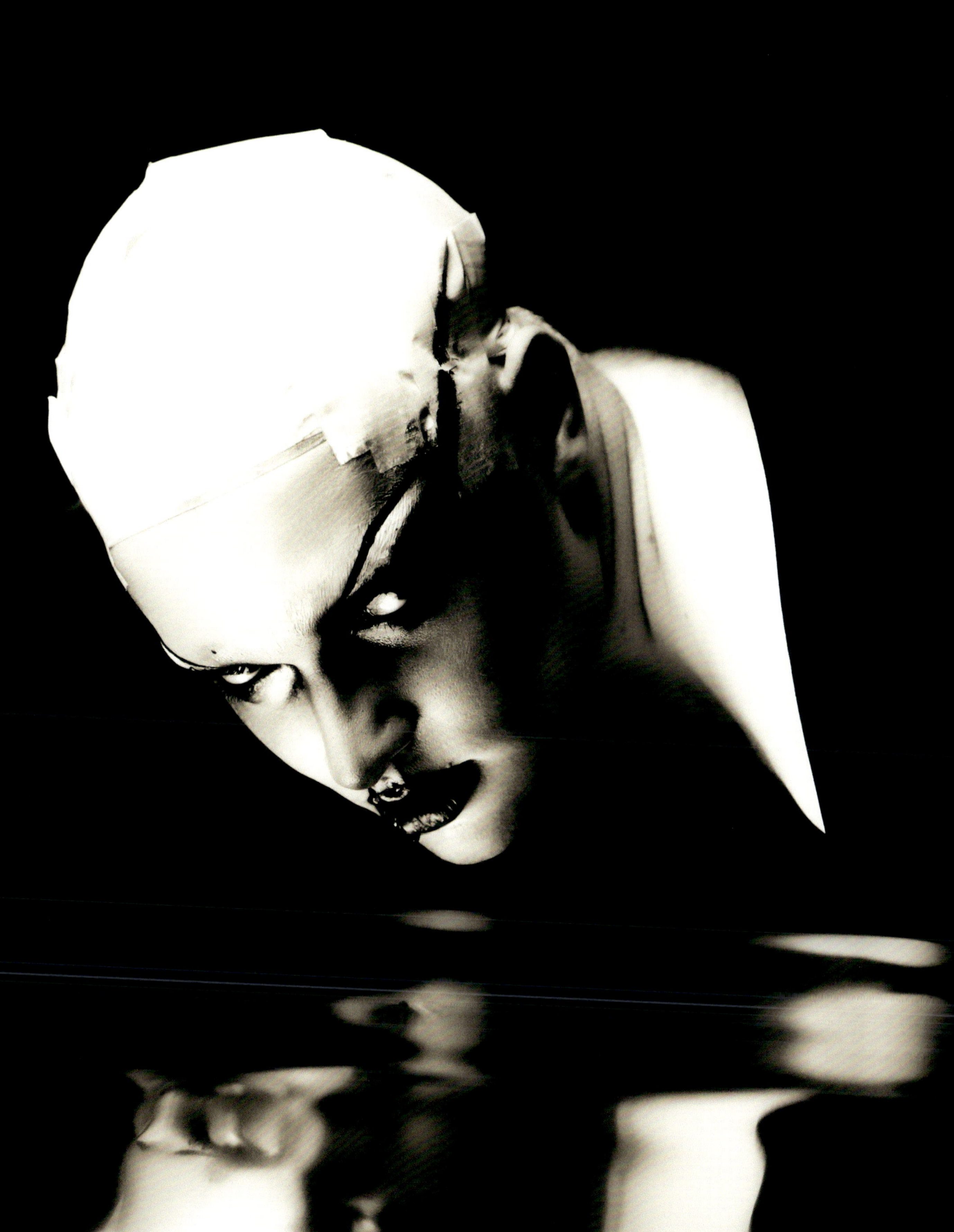

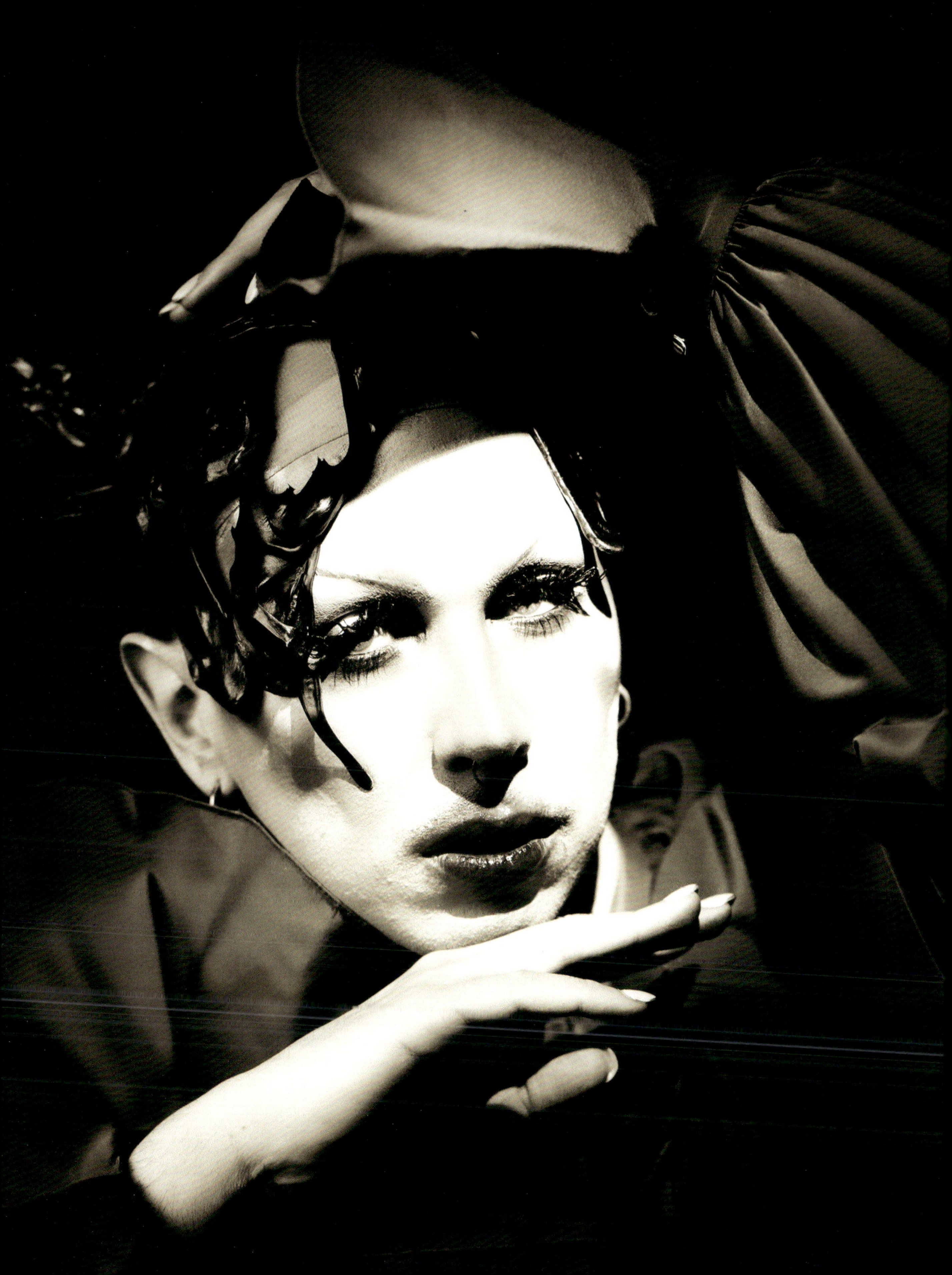

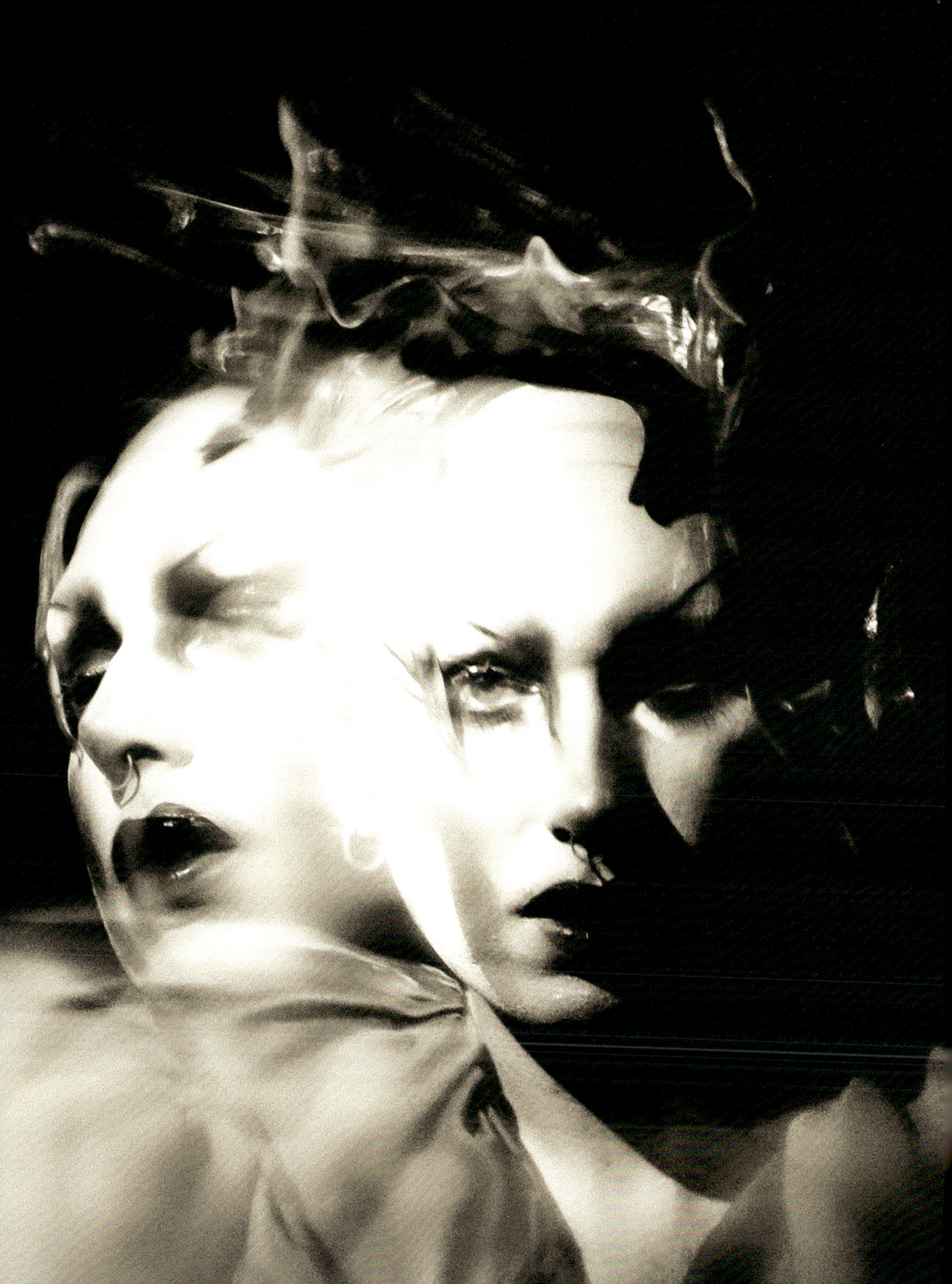

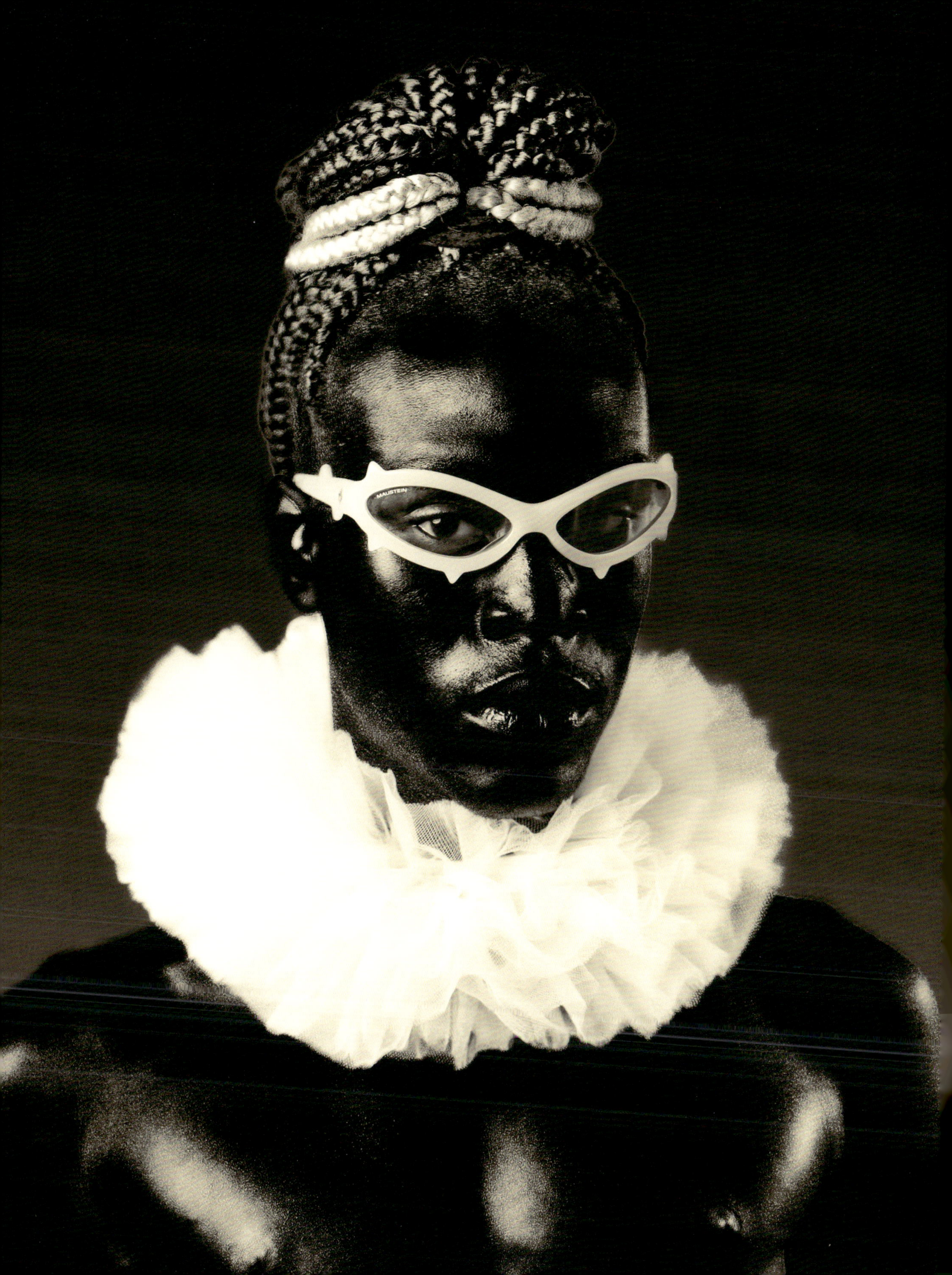
MAUSTEIN

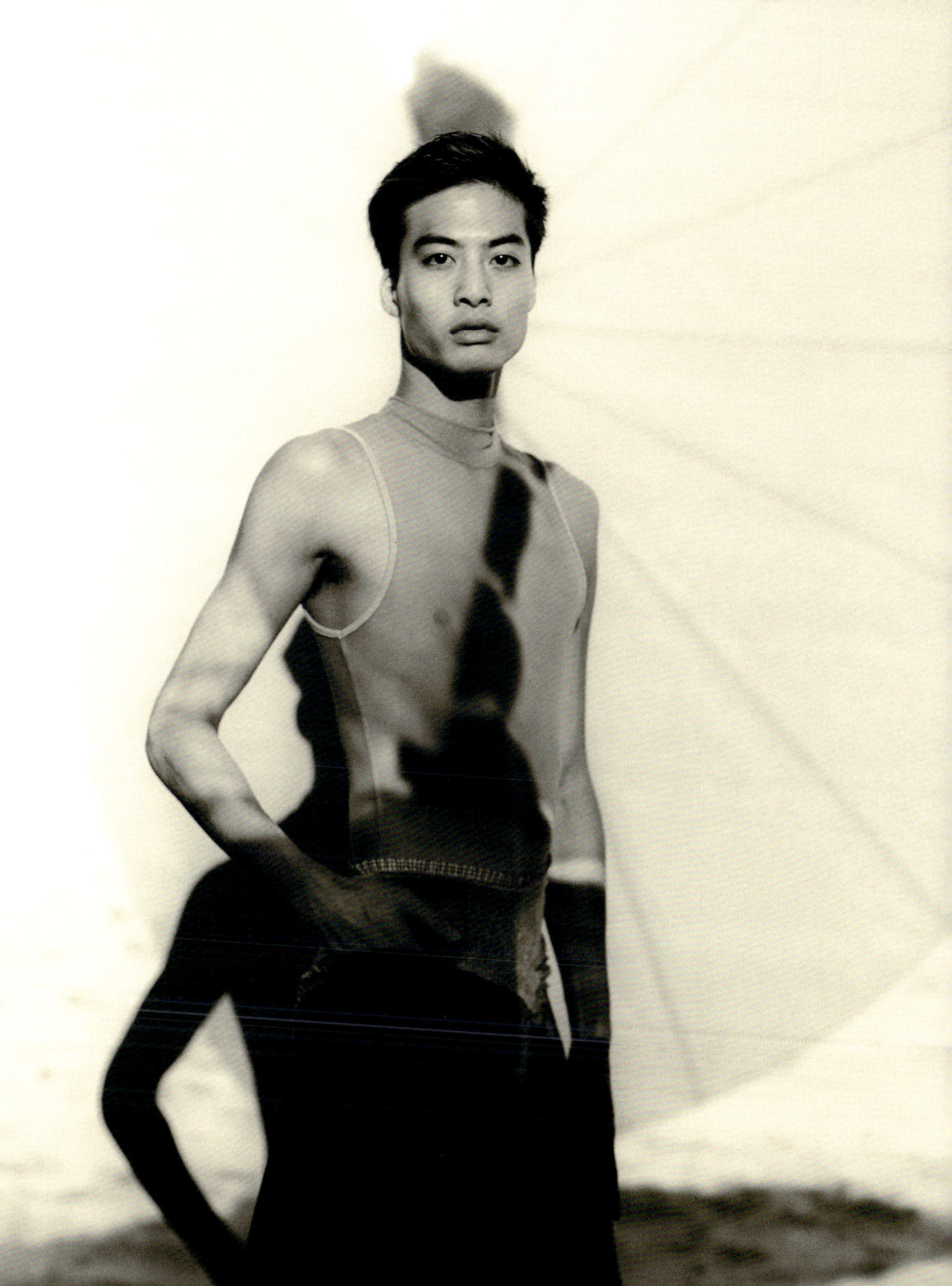

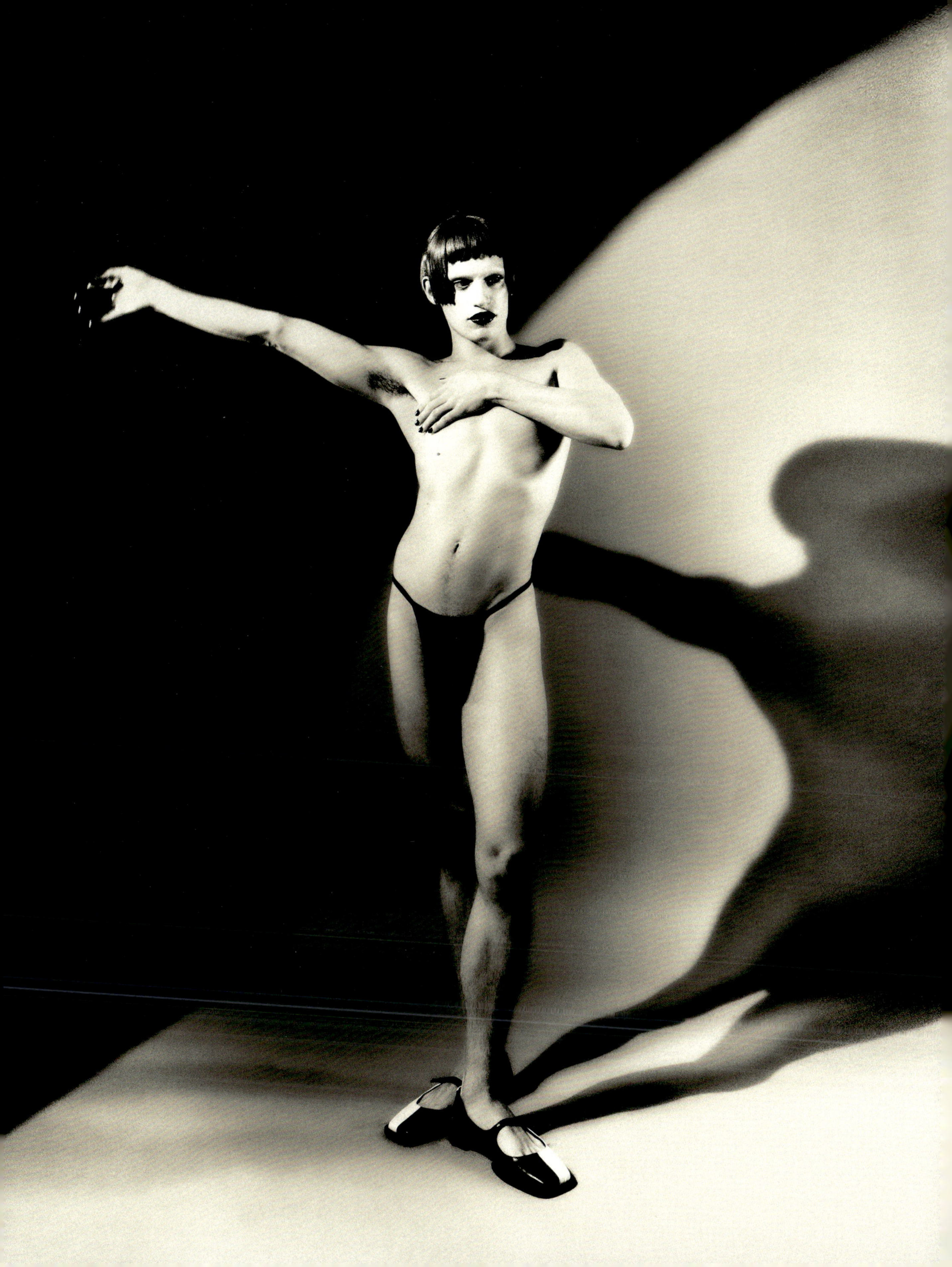

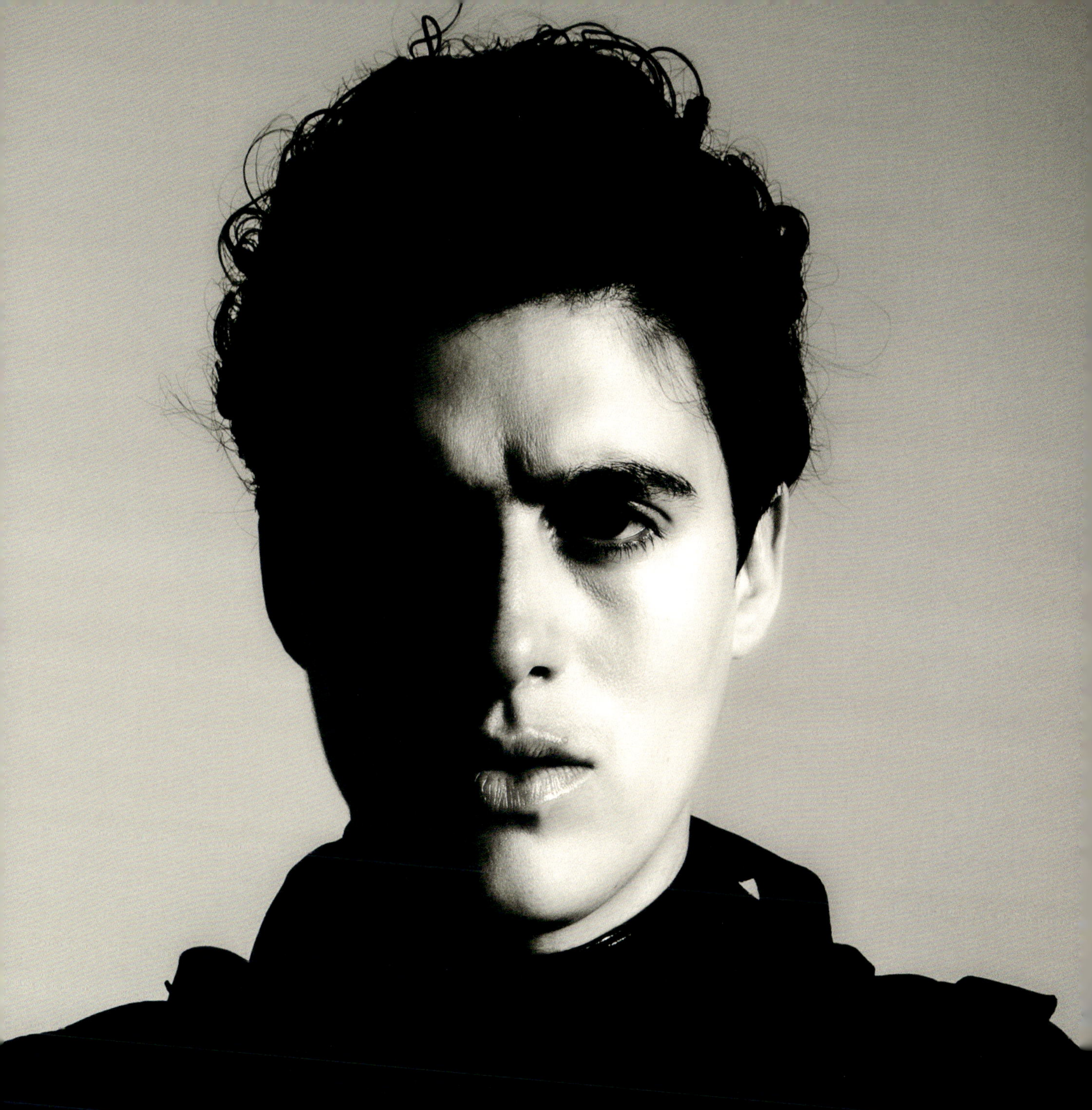

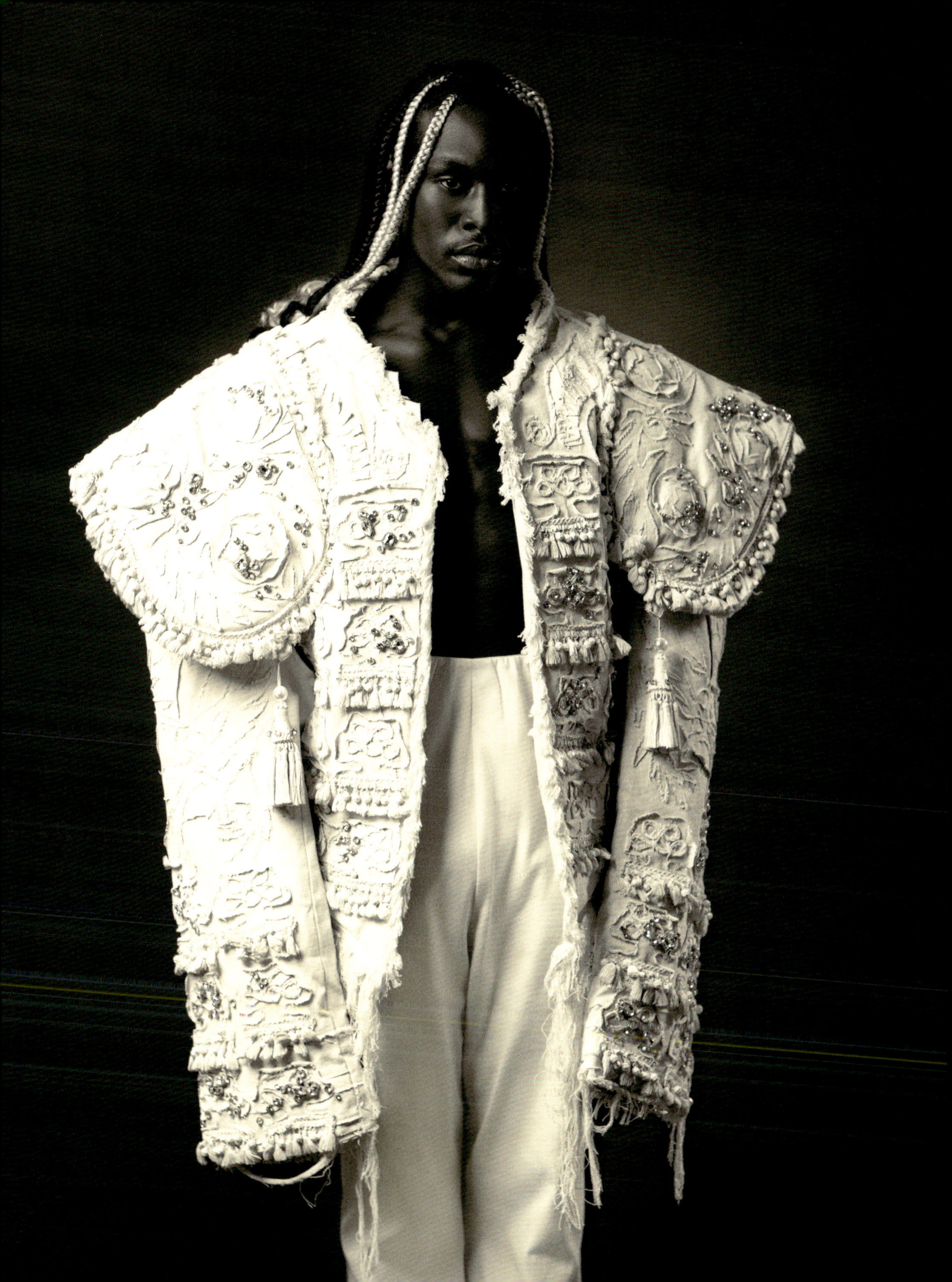

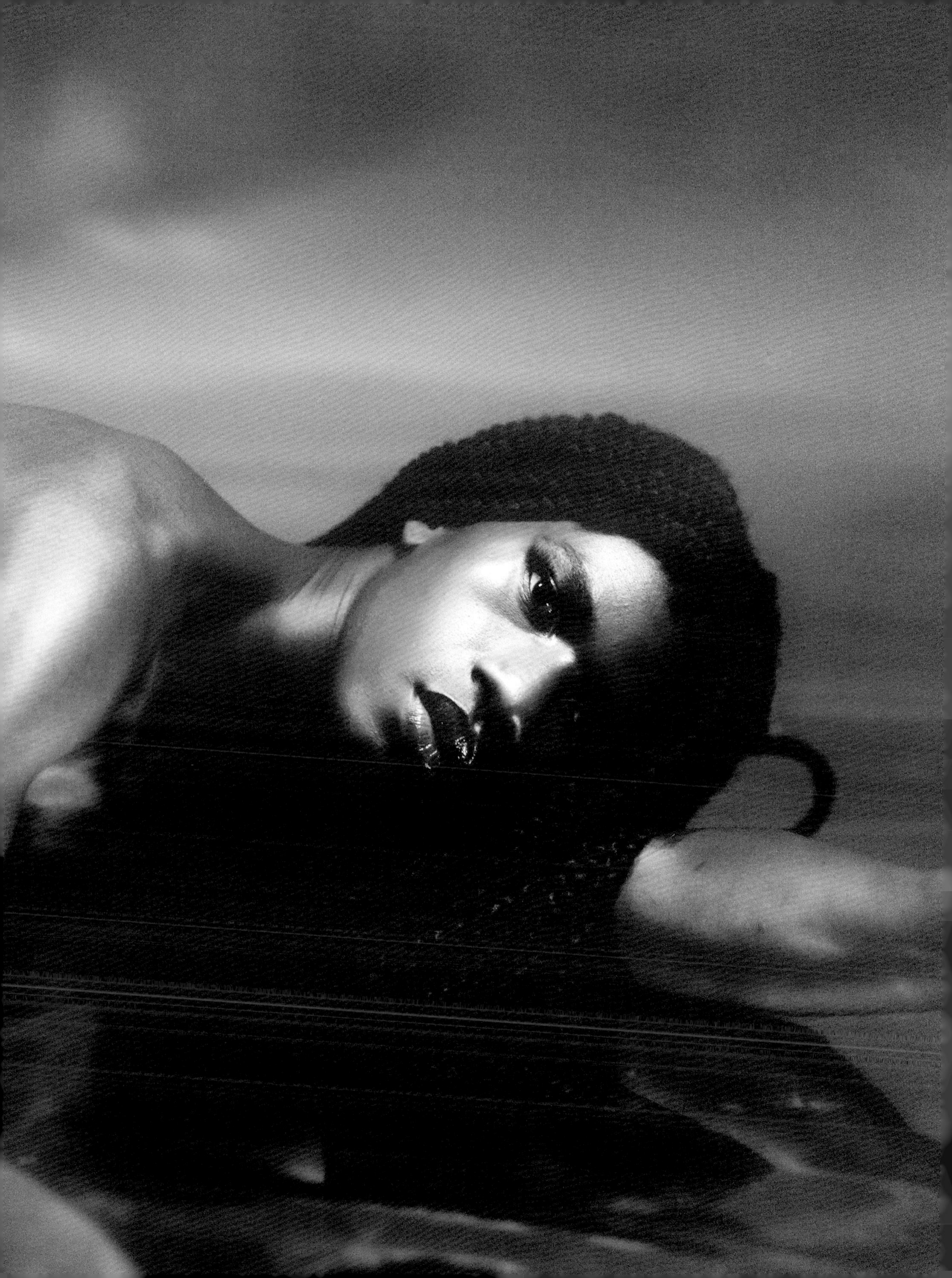

Editorials

The photographs presented here are editorial works that I have created in collaboration with various magazines and campaigns that specifically center the queer community. For me, these images are far more than commissions; they signify a continuation of my photographic journey, a journey that began in the most intimate of spaces: my own living room.

It started with a self-initiated project titled "Immigrants," where I invited people from our community into my home to co-create images that authentically reflected our shared experiences and need for self-expression. This fundamental impulse—to create out of necessity, driven by a deep need to connect and represent—ultimately opened the doors to these editorial collaborations. They served not only as a form of recognition but also as a powerful continuation of my desire to make vital space for authenticity and beauty within the queer narrative.

I hope you will find that each image within this collection holds on to that original spirit. Even when working within the frameworks of campaigns or facing editorial constraints, I tried to remain firmly grounded in my core vision and, if I succeeded, it is largely thanks to the tremendous trust of the individuals I photograph and the dedicated teams of artists I've had the privilege to work with.

The very elements you see—the vibrant colors, the carefully chosen environments, and the evocative gestures—all speak to a shared language of creativity and care that underpinned each session. I am immensely proud of this work and profoundly grateful to the people and publications who have openly supported our unique perspective, and need for a space to express our queerness.

Above all, my deepest thanks go to the incredible collaborators who brought these visions to life. Each and every shoot has been a true celebration of queer presence, expression, and solidarity, directly emphasizing the collaborative and community-driven nature of this work.

—ASAFE

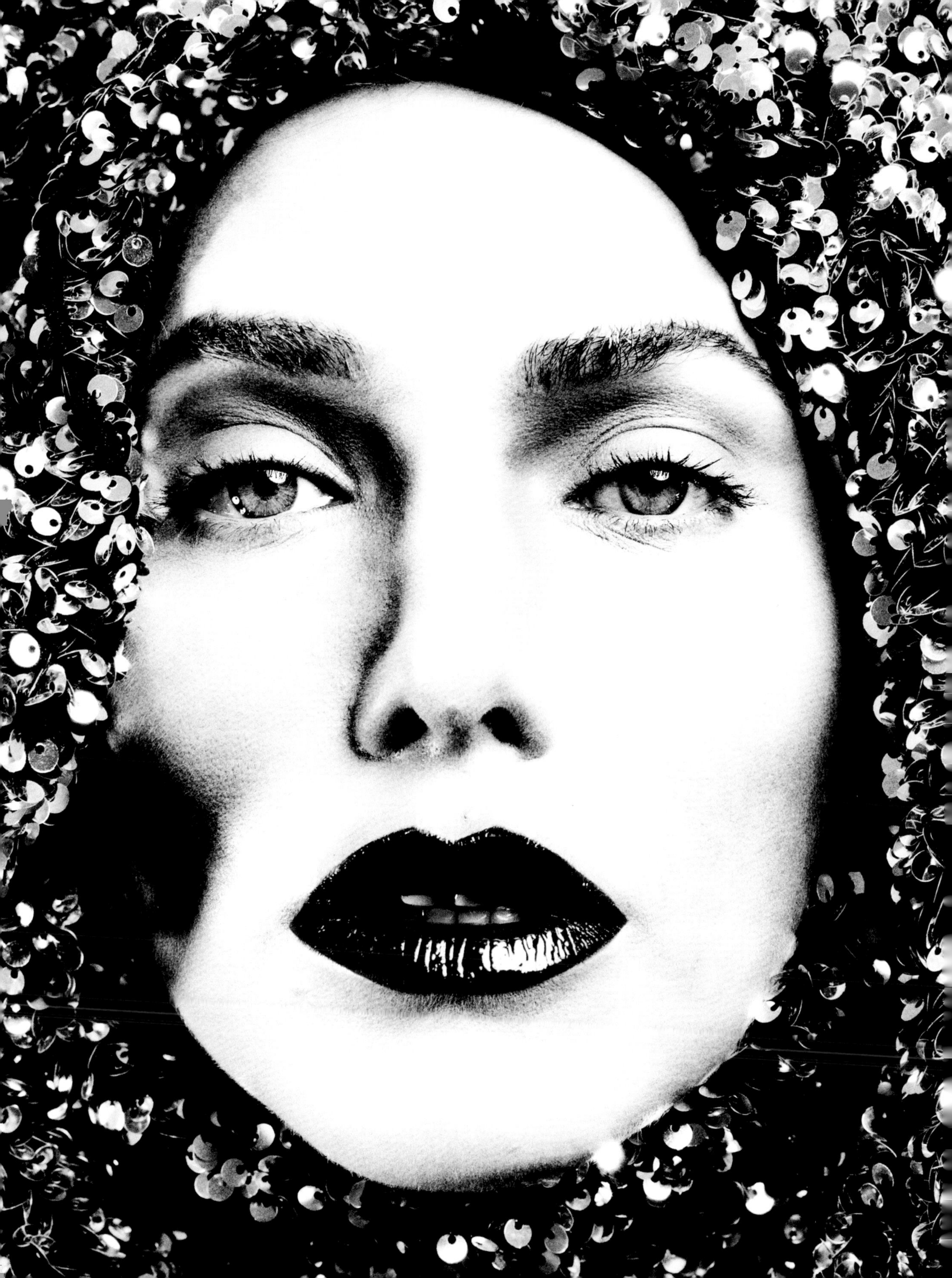

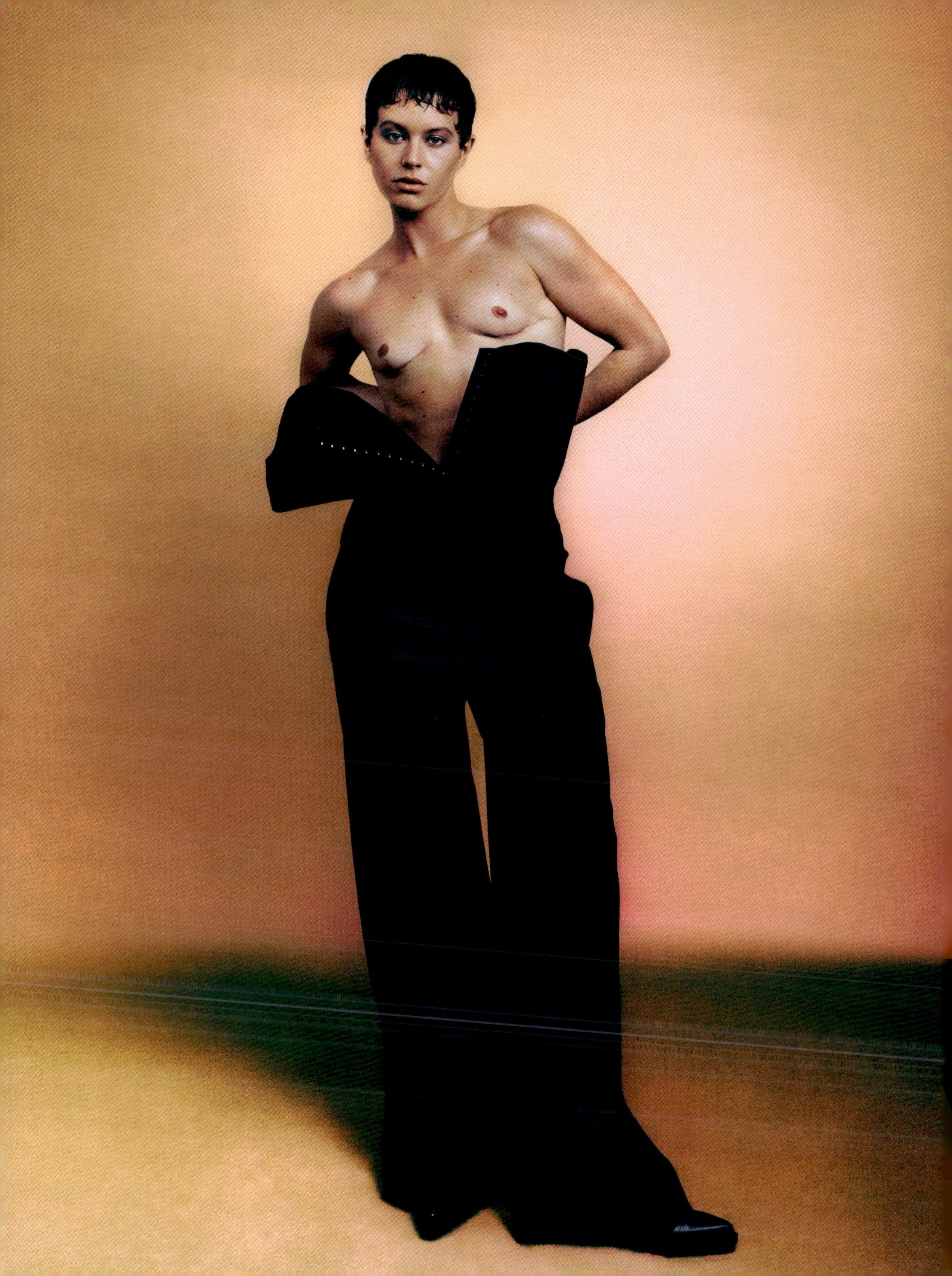

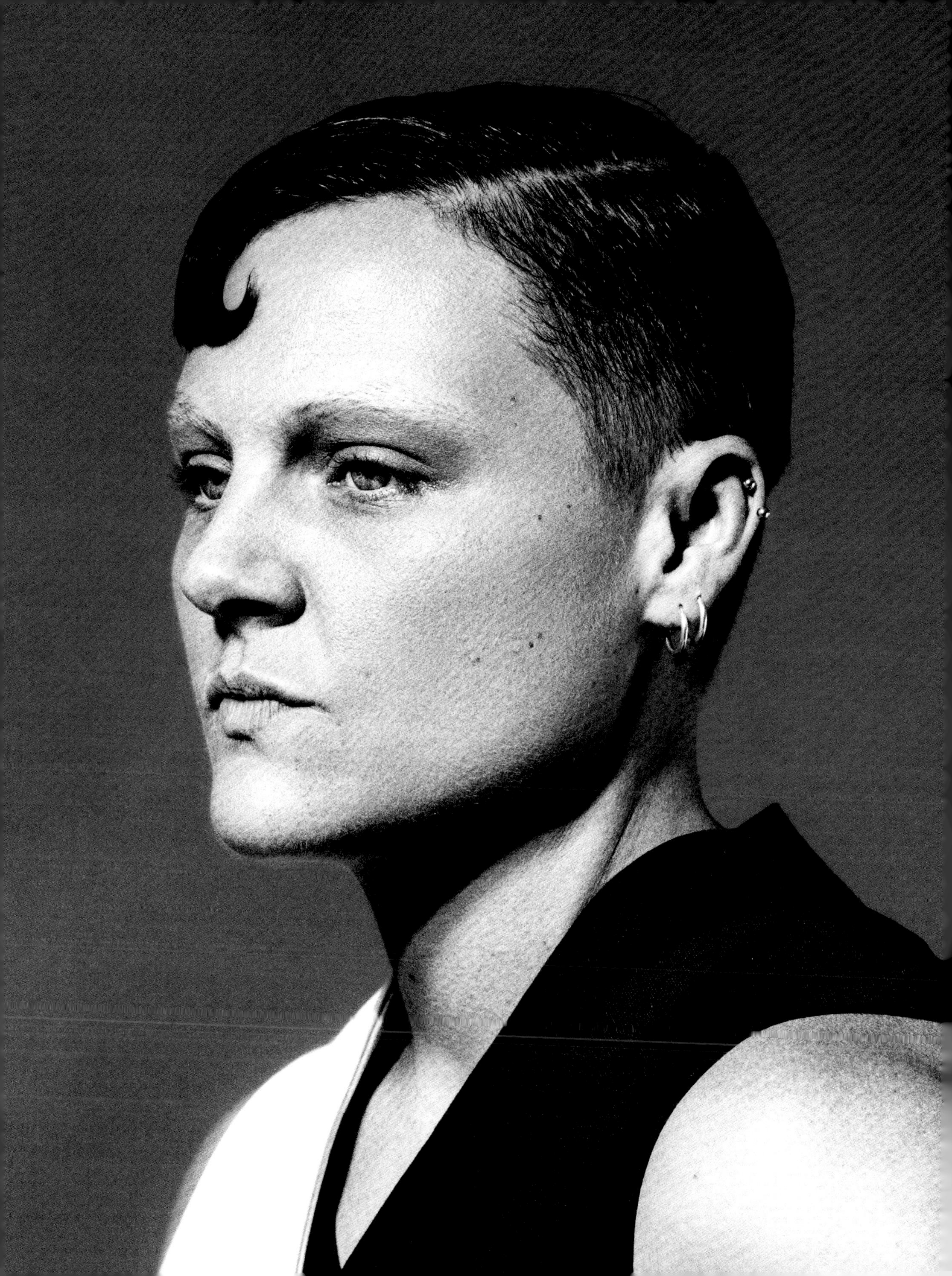

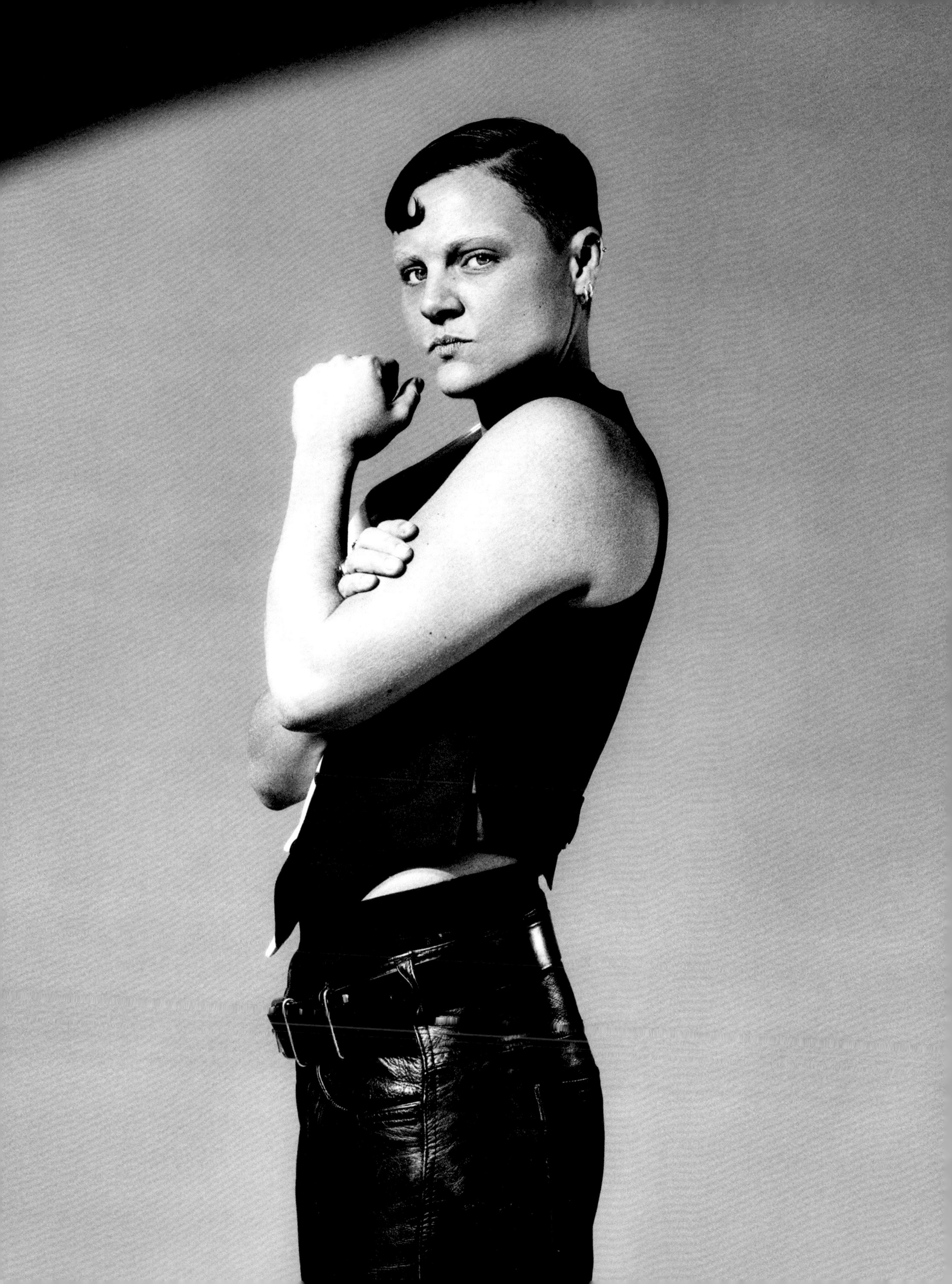

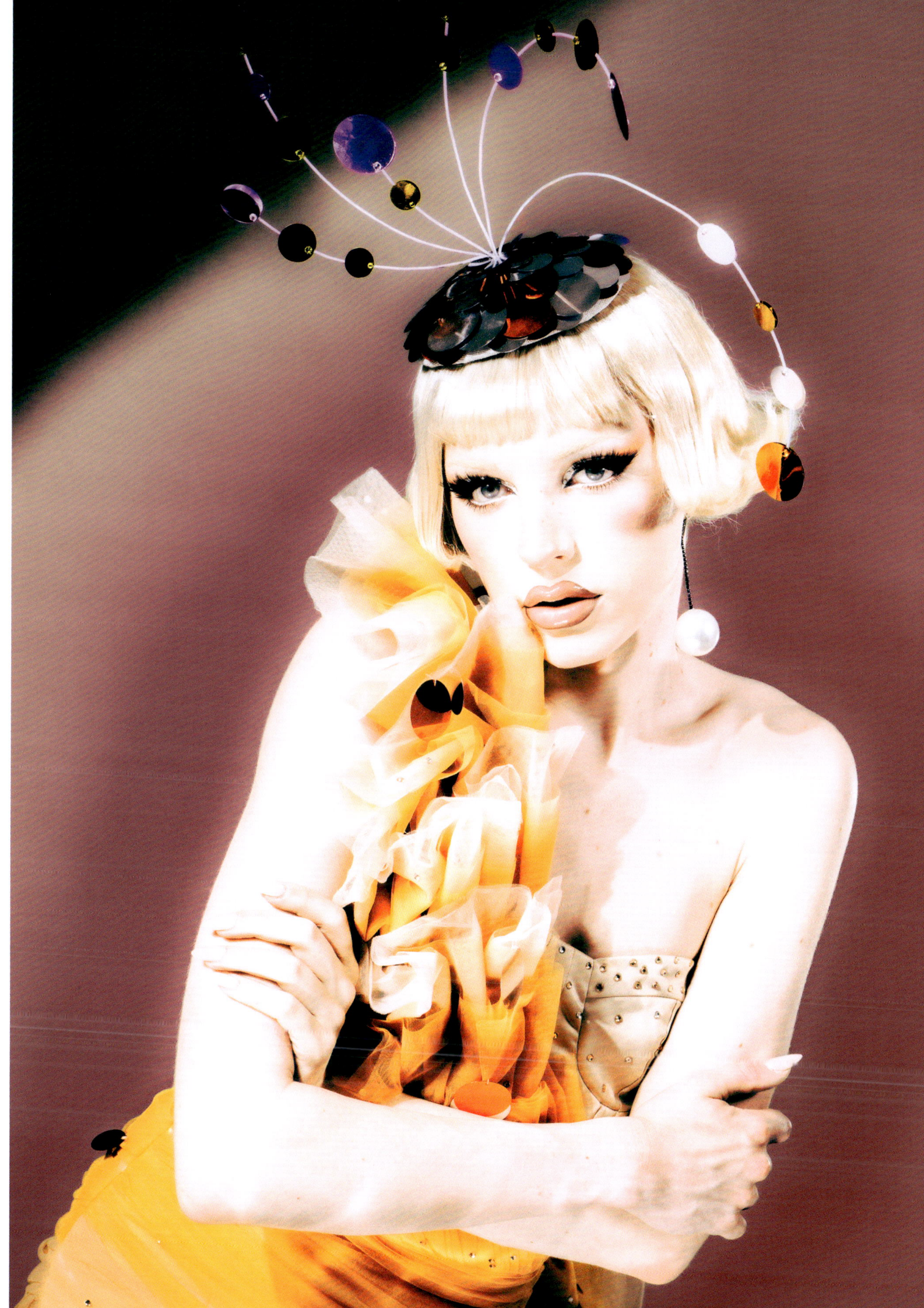

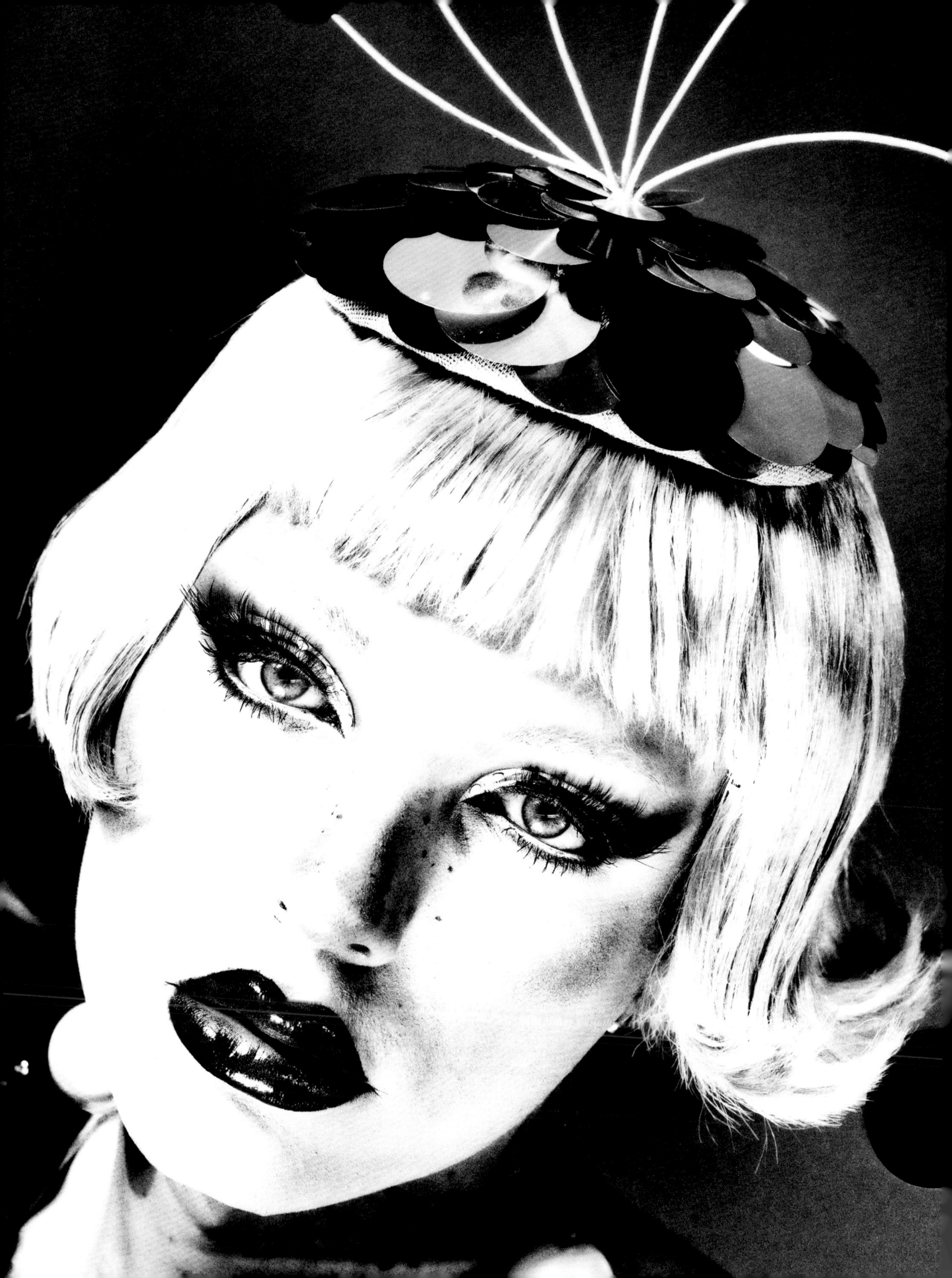

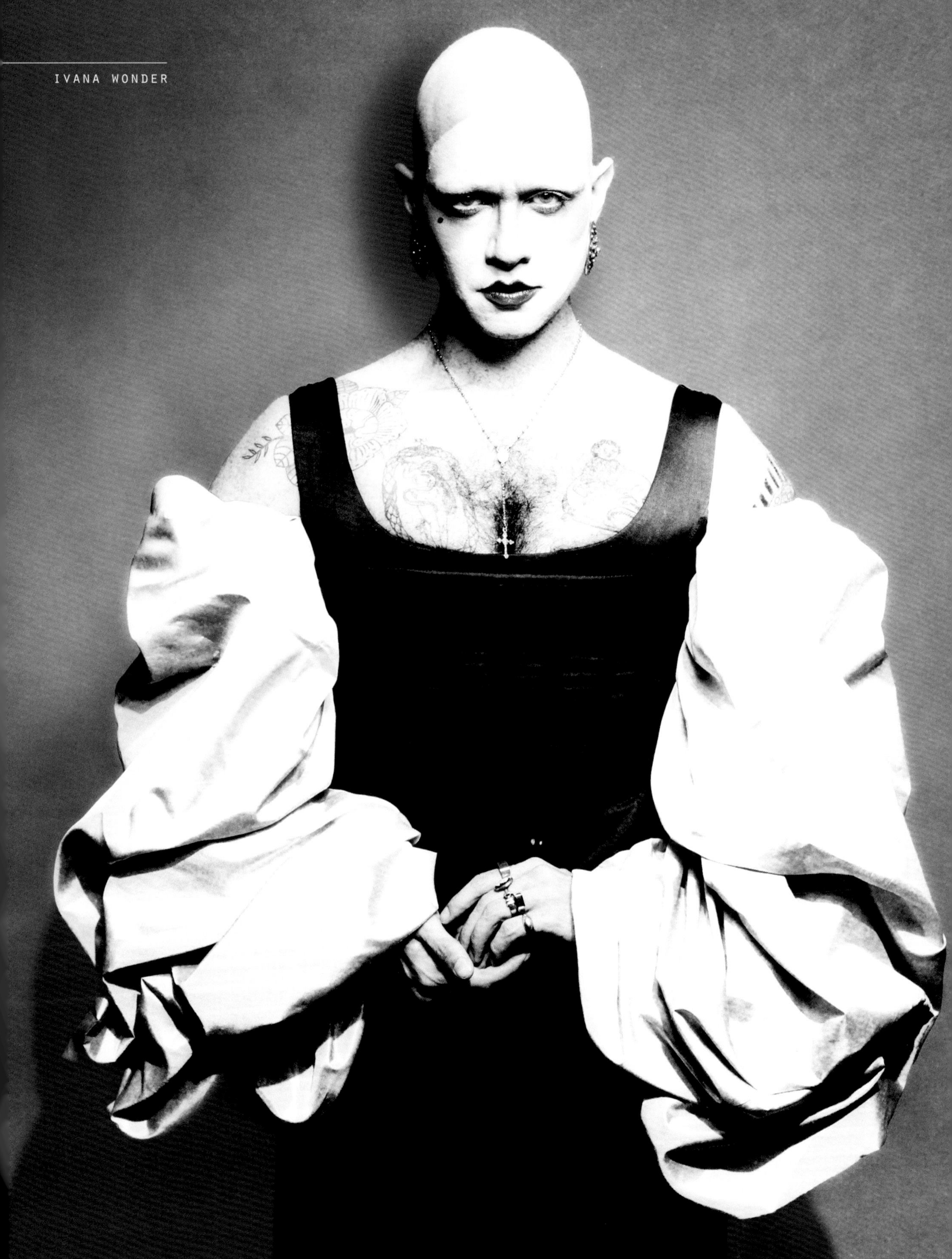
IVANA WONDER

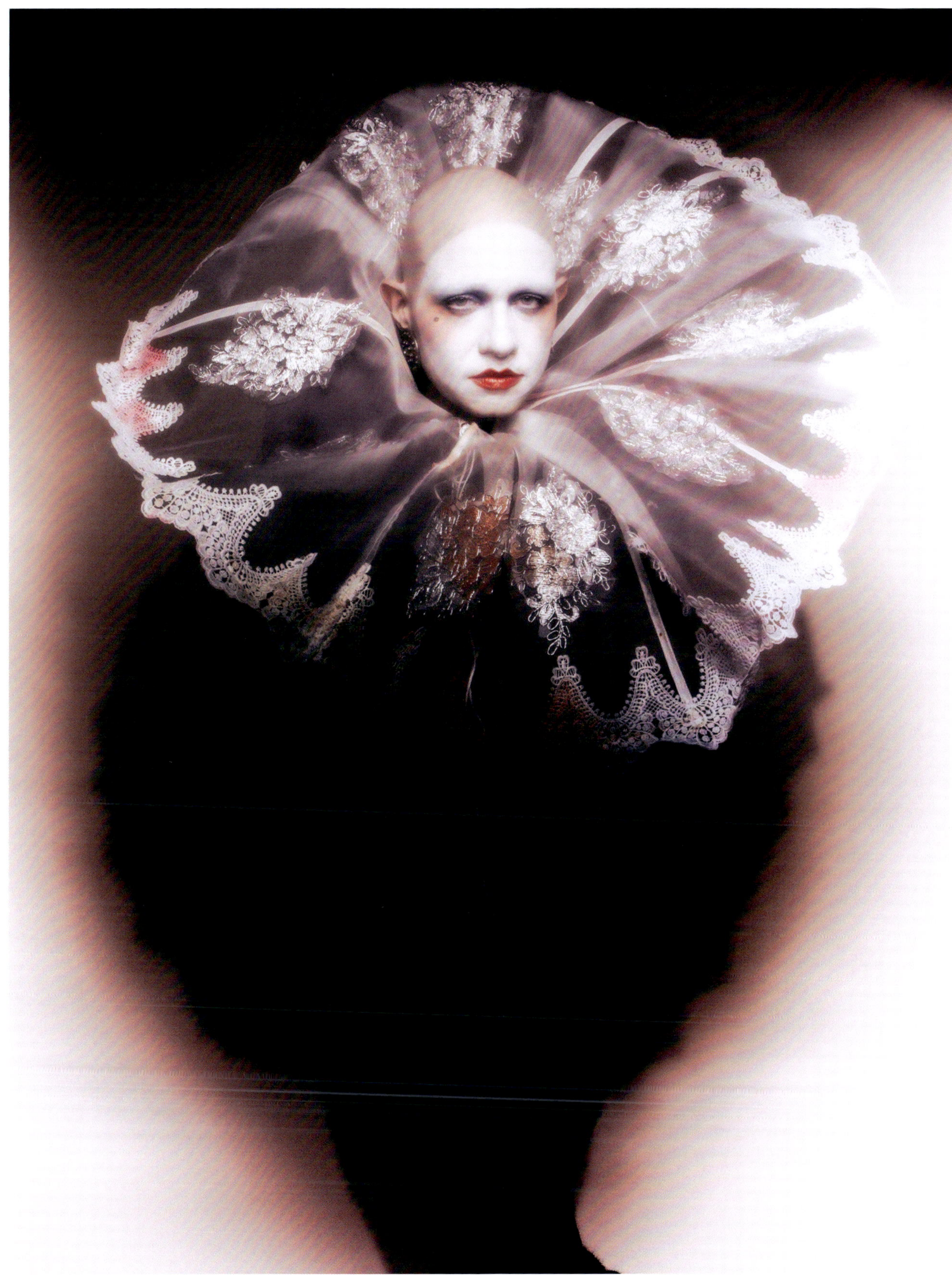

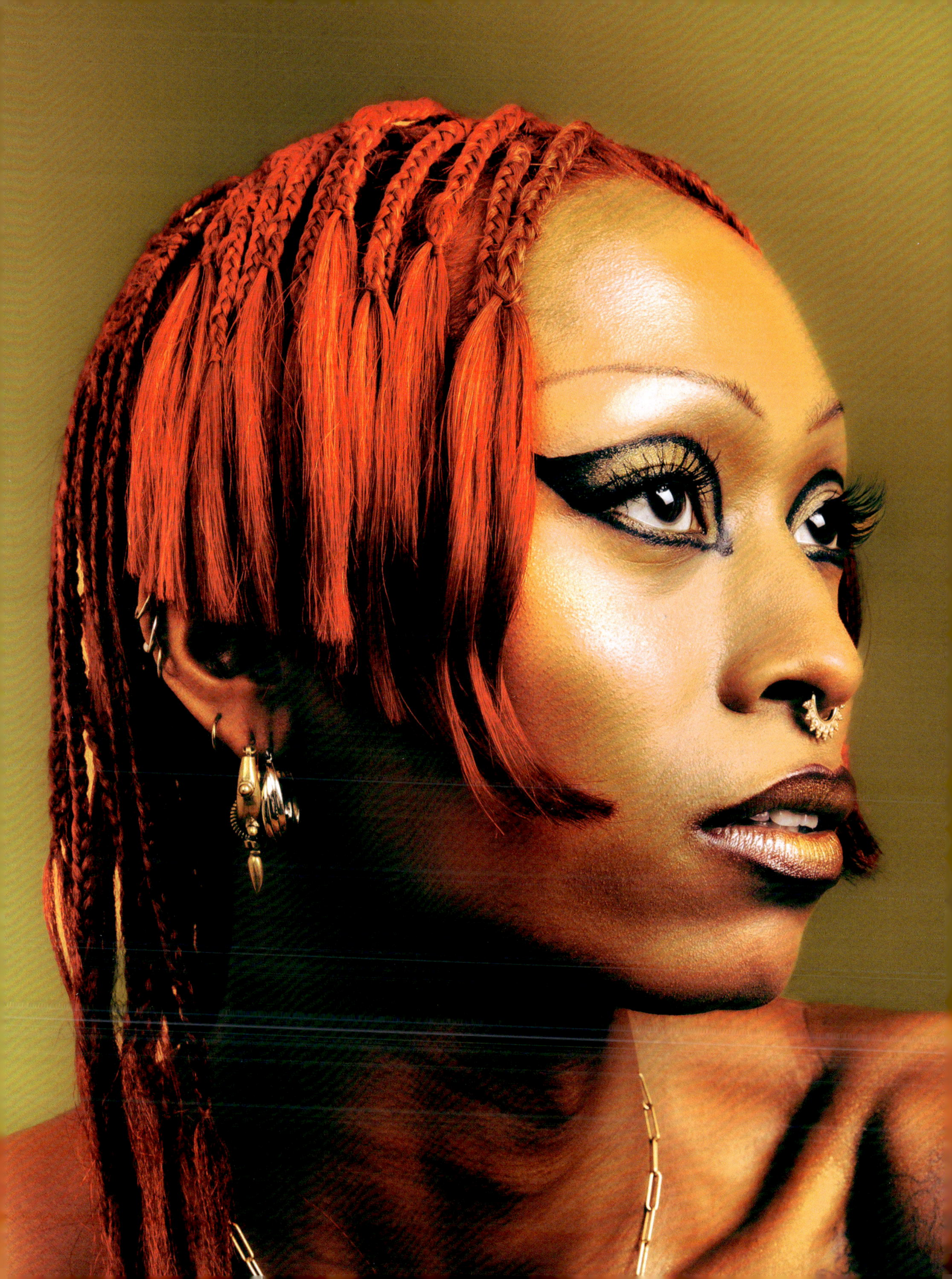

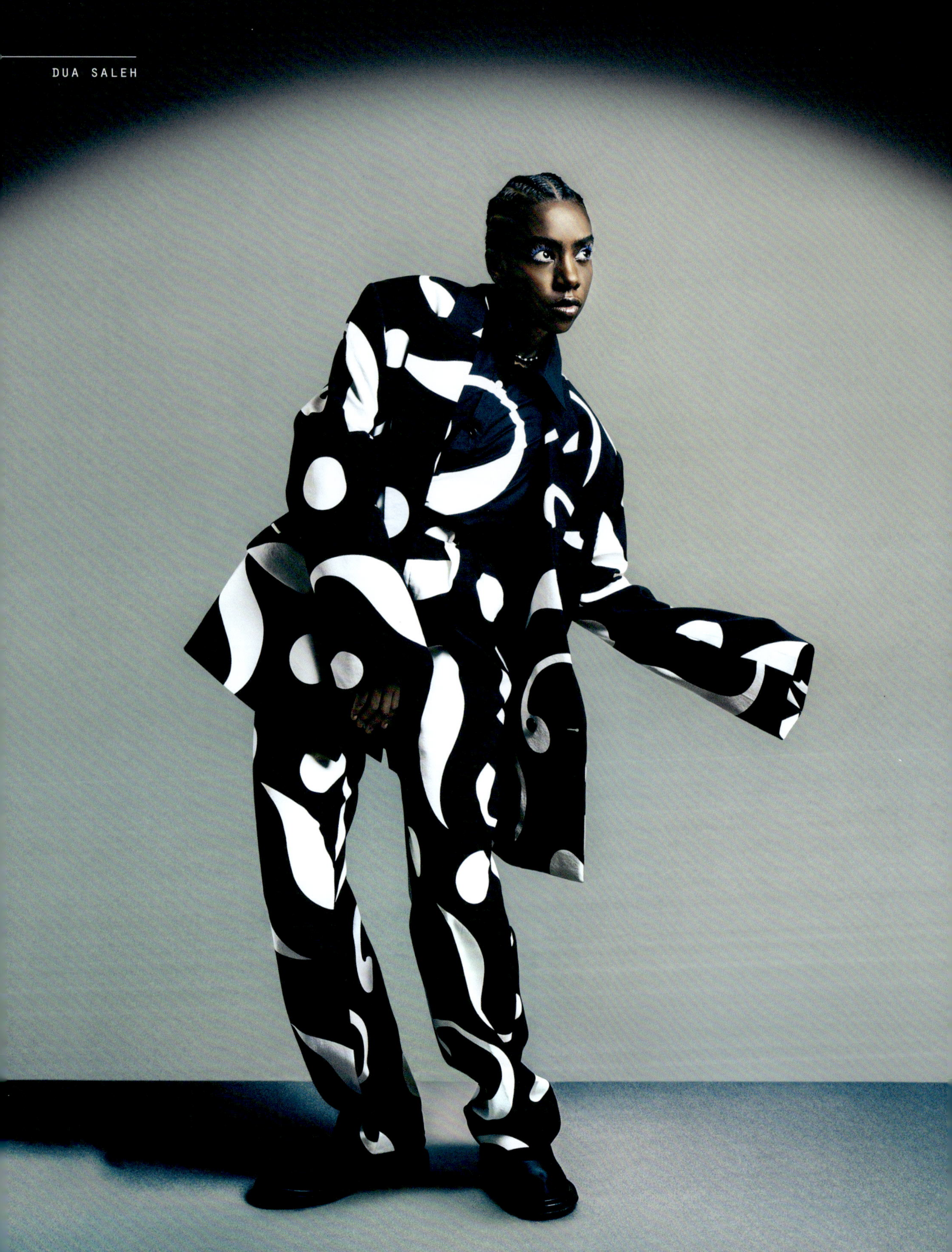

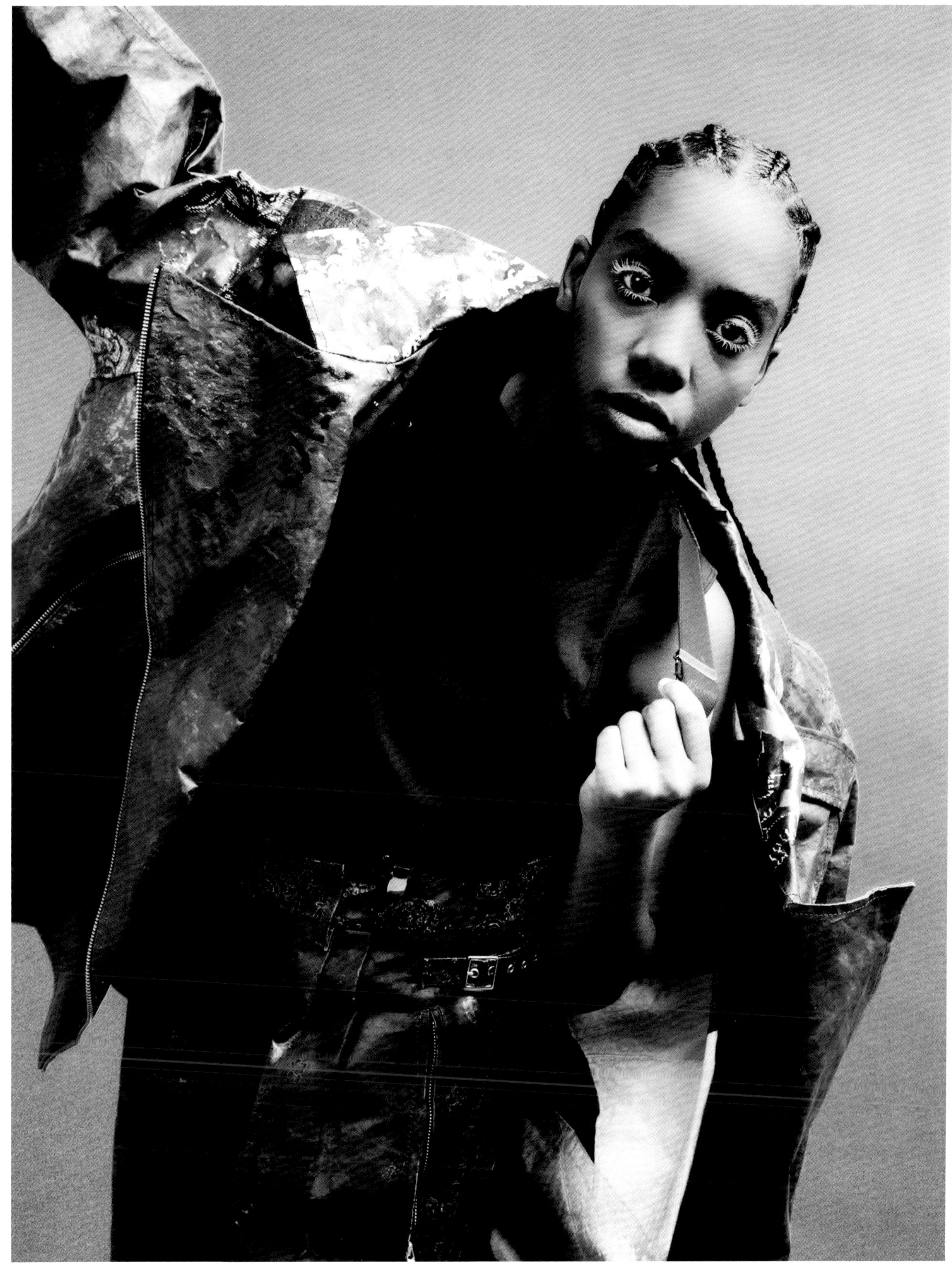

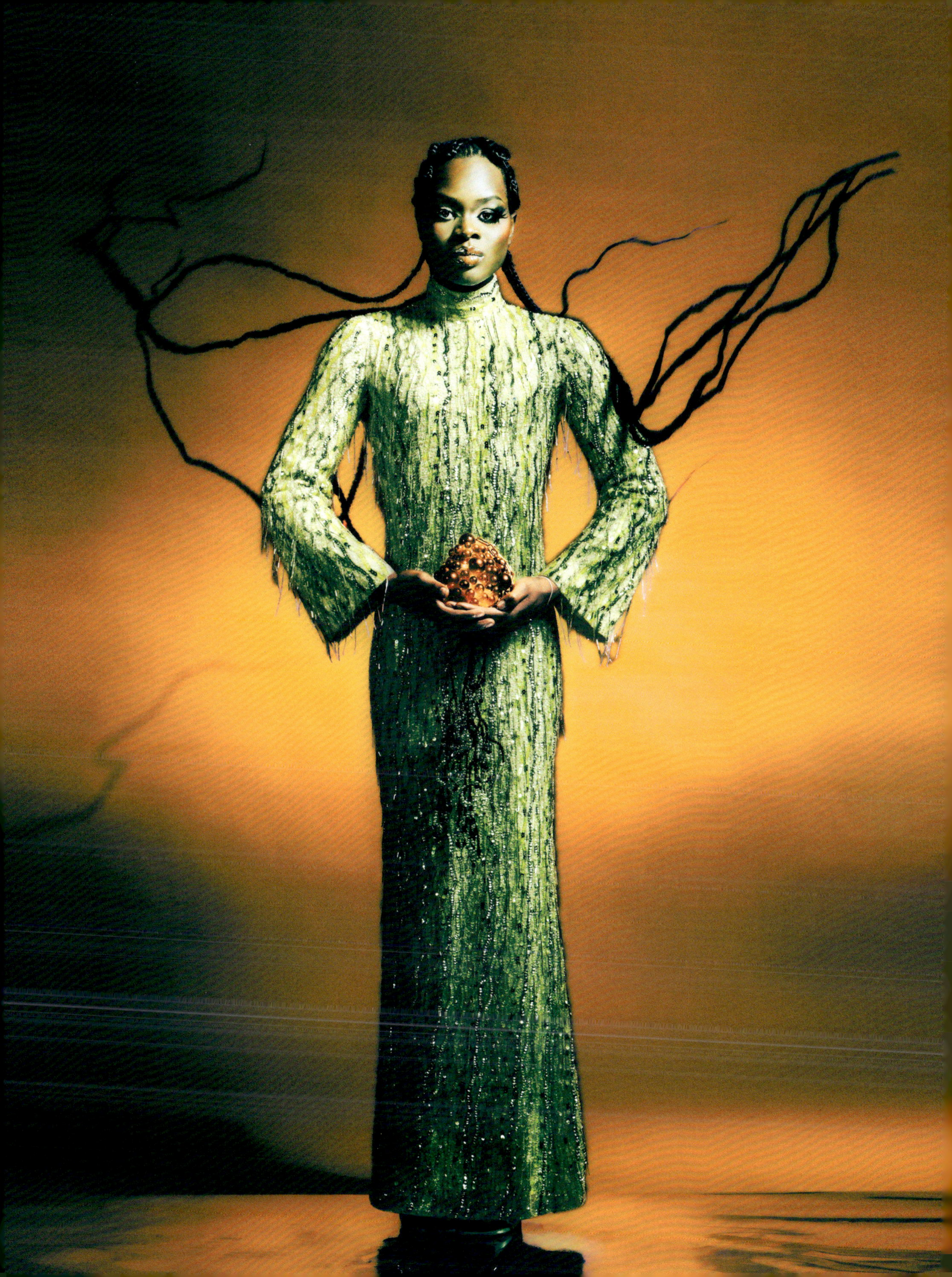

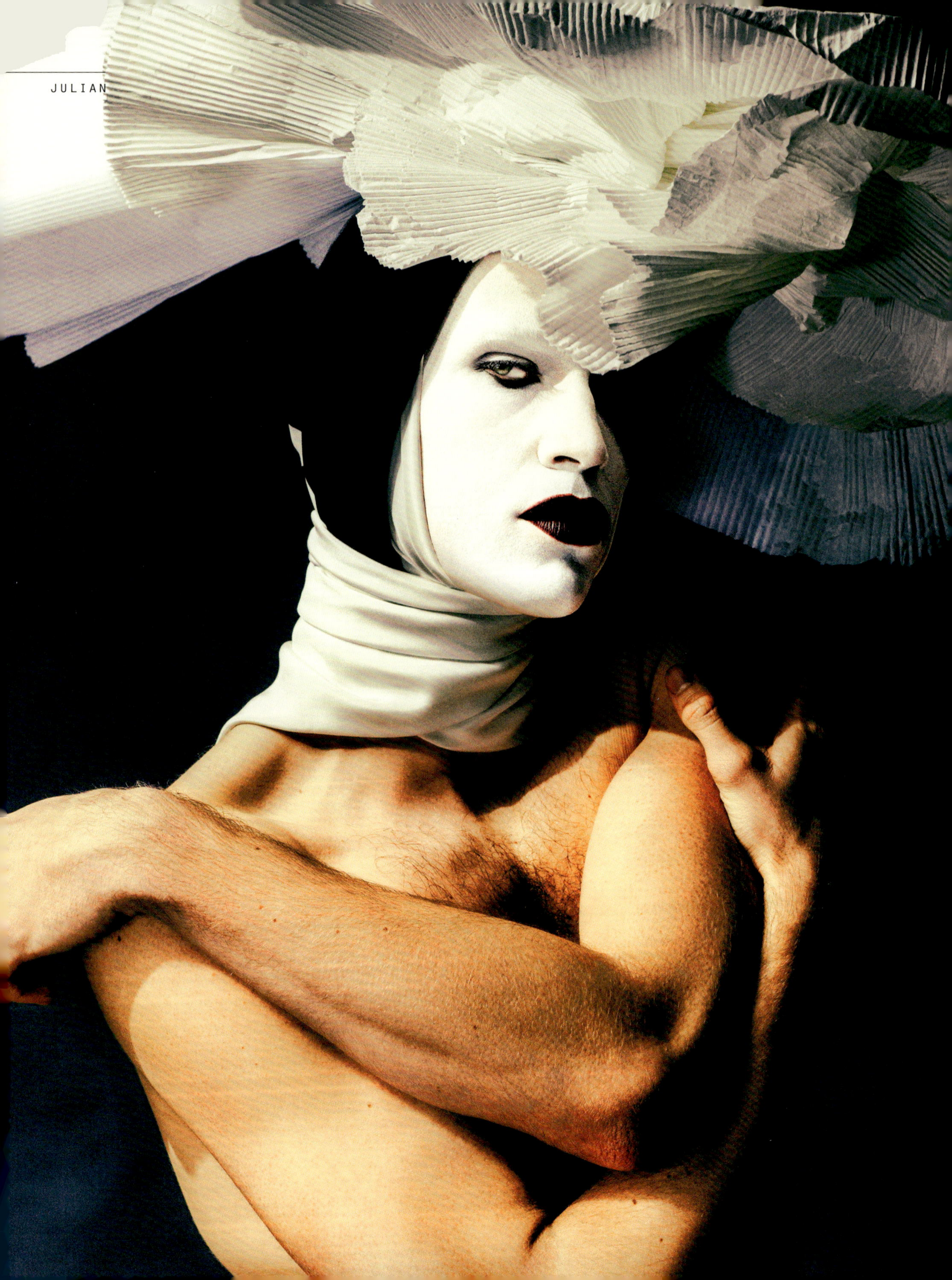

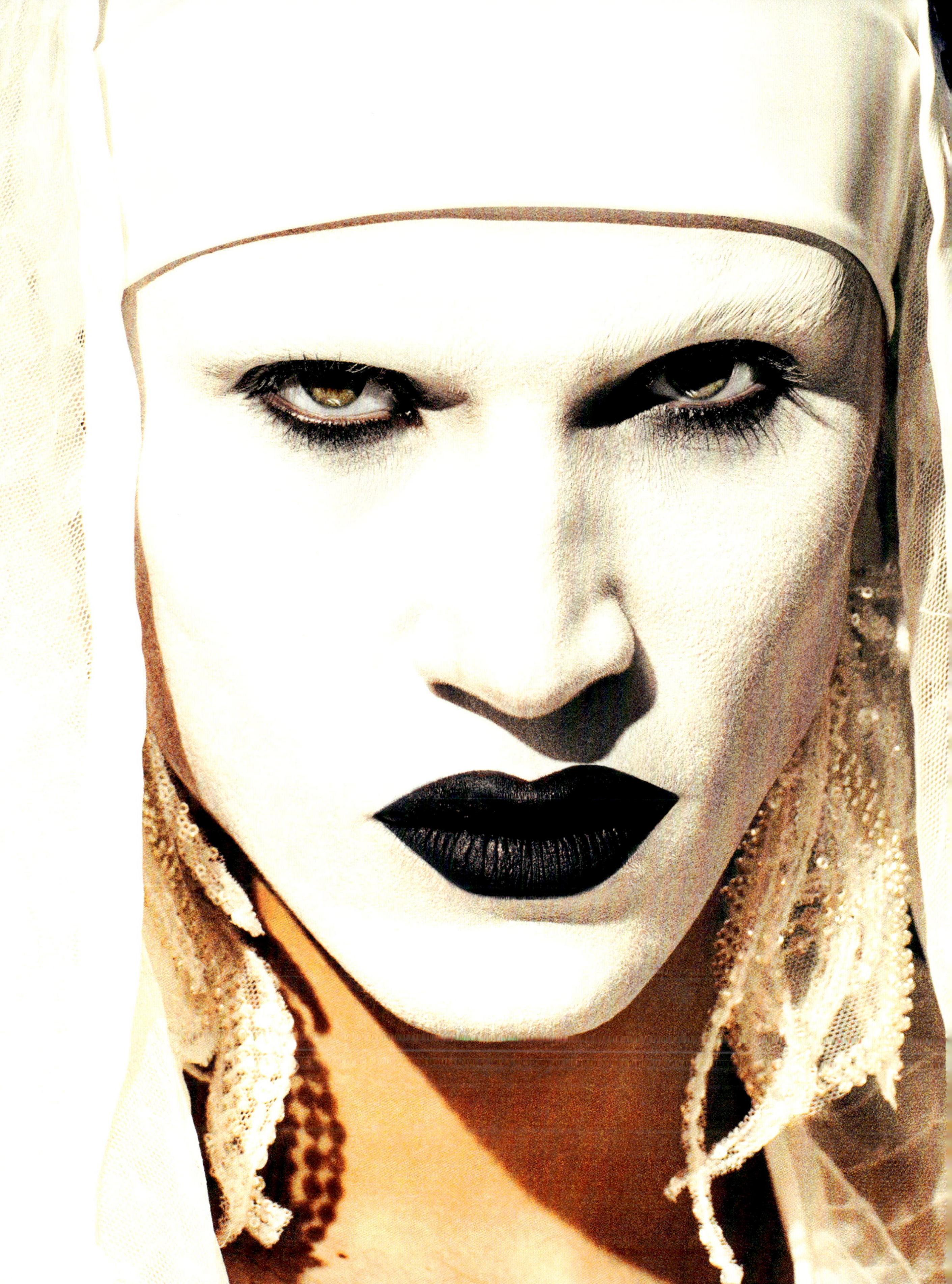

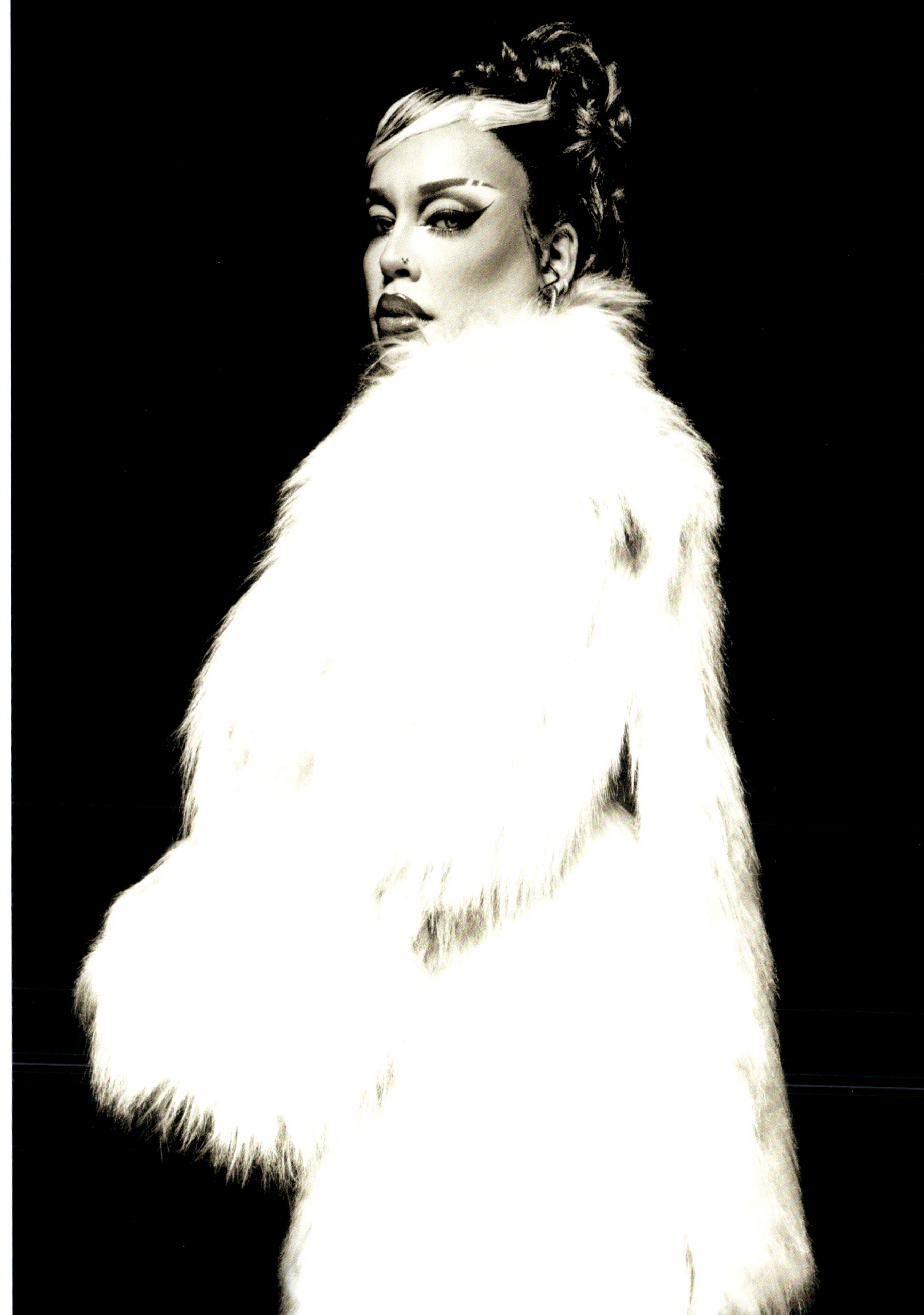

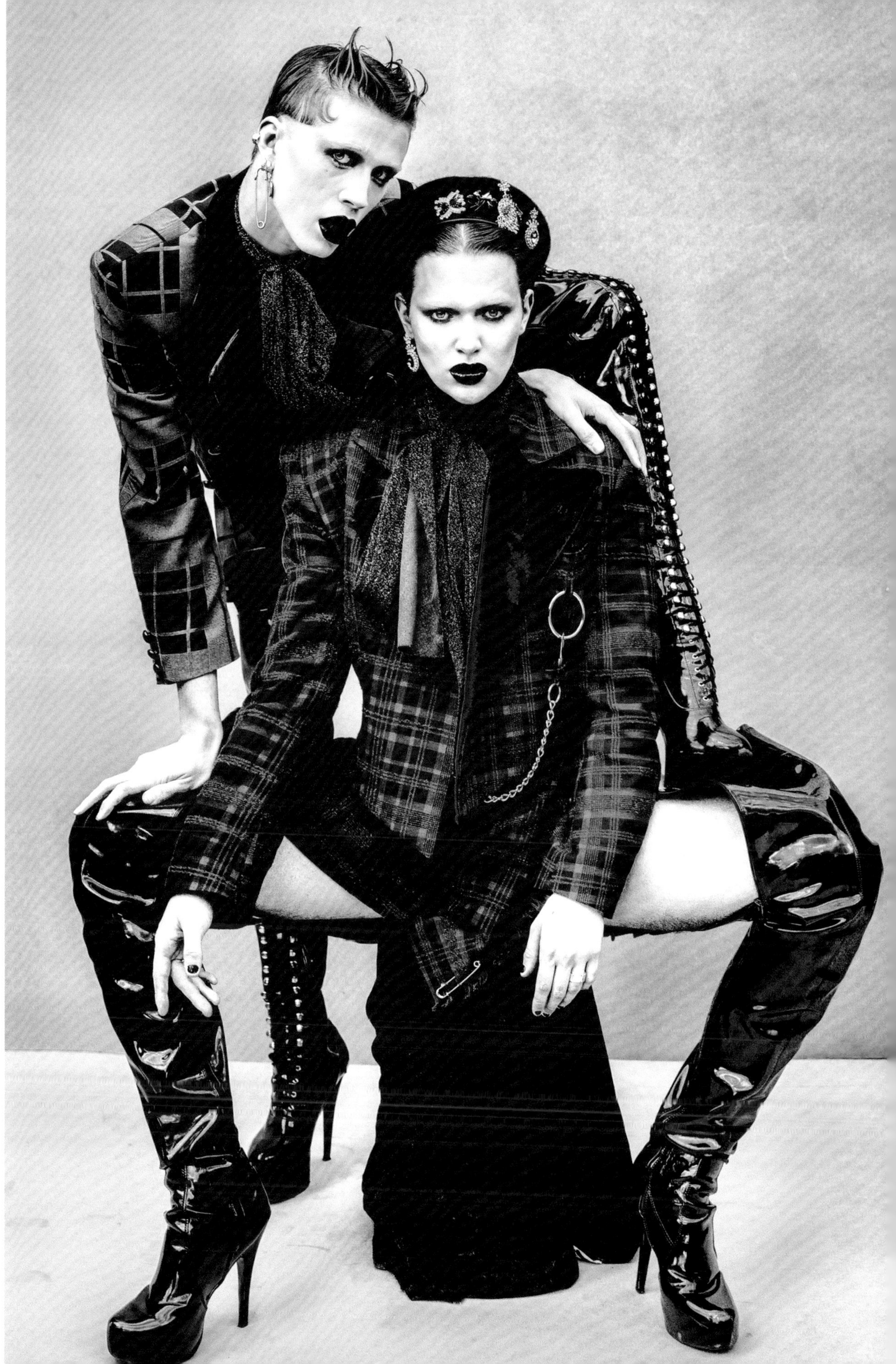

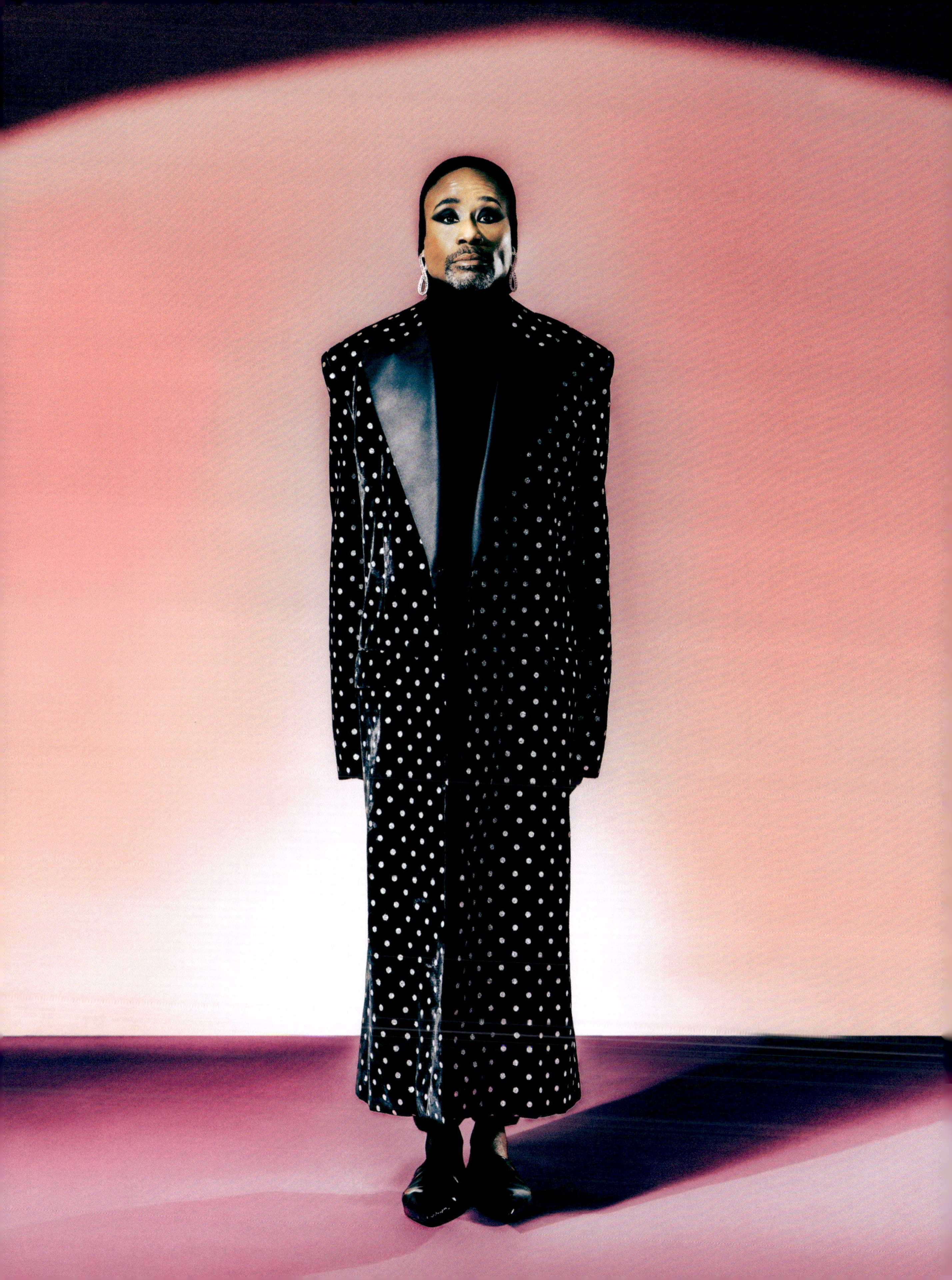

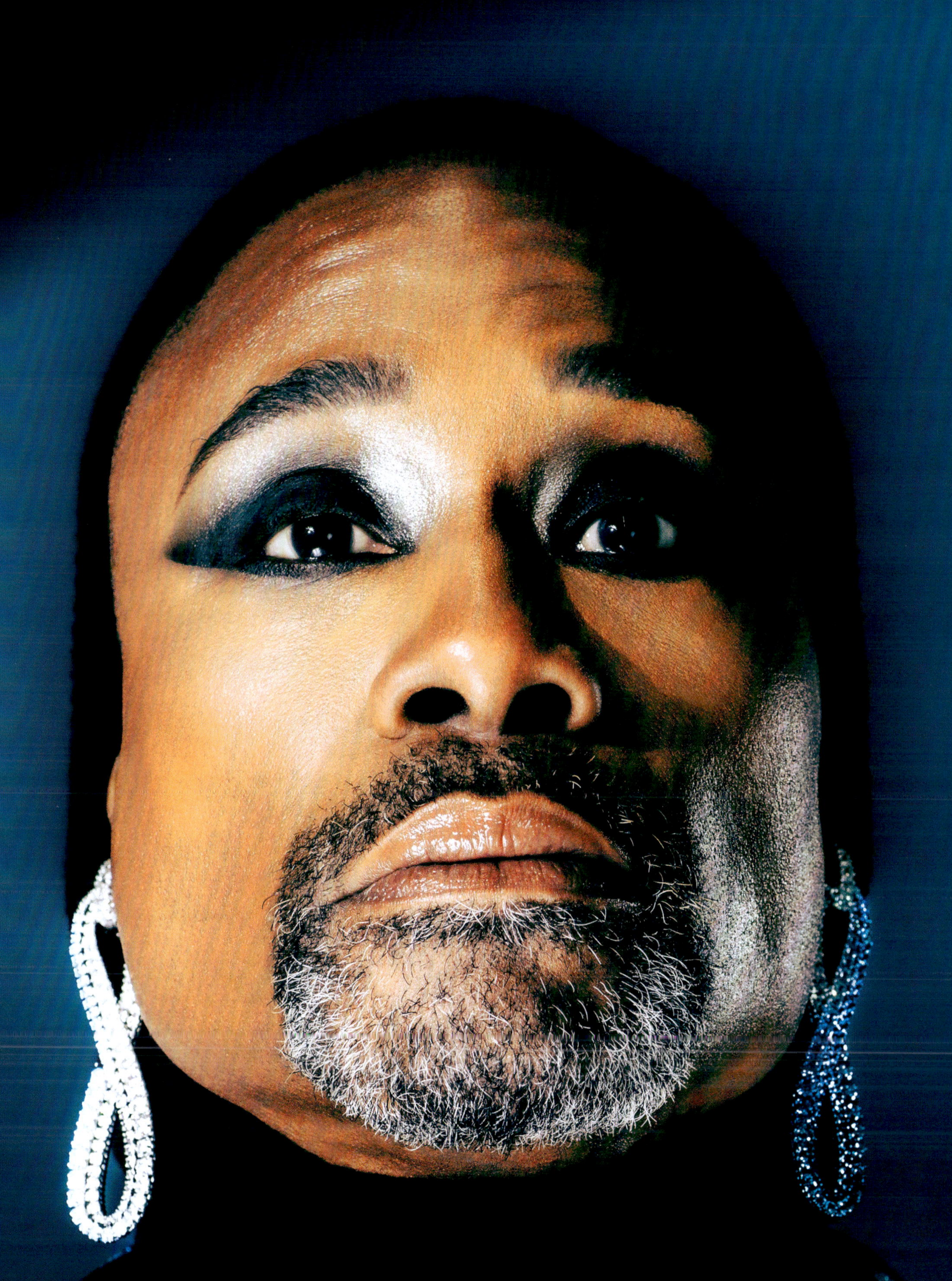

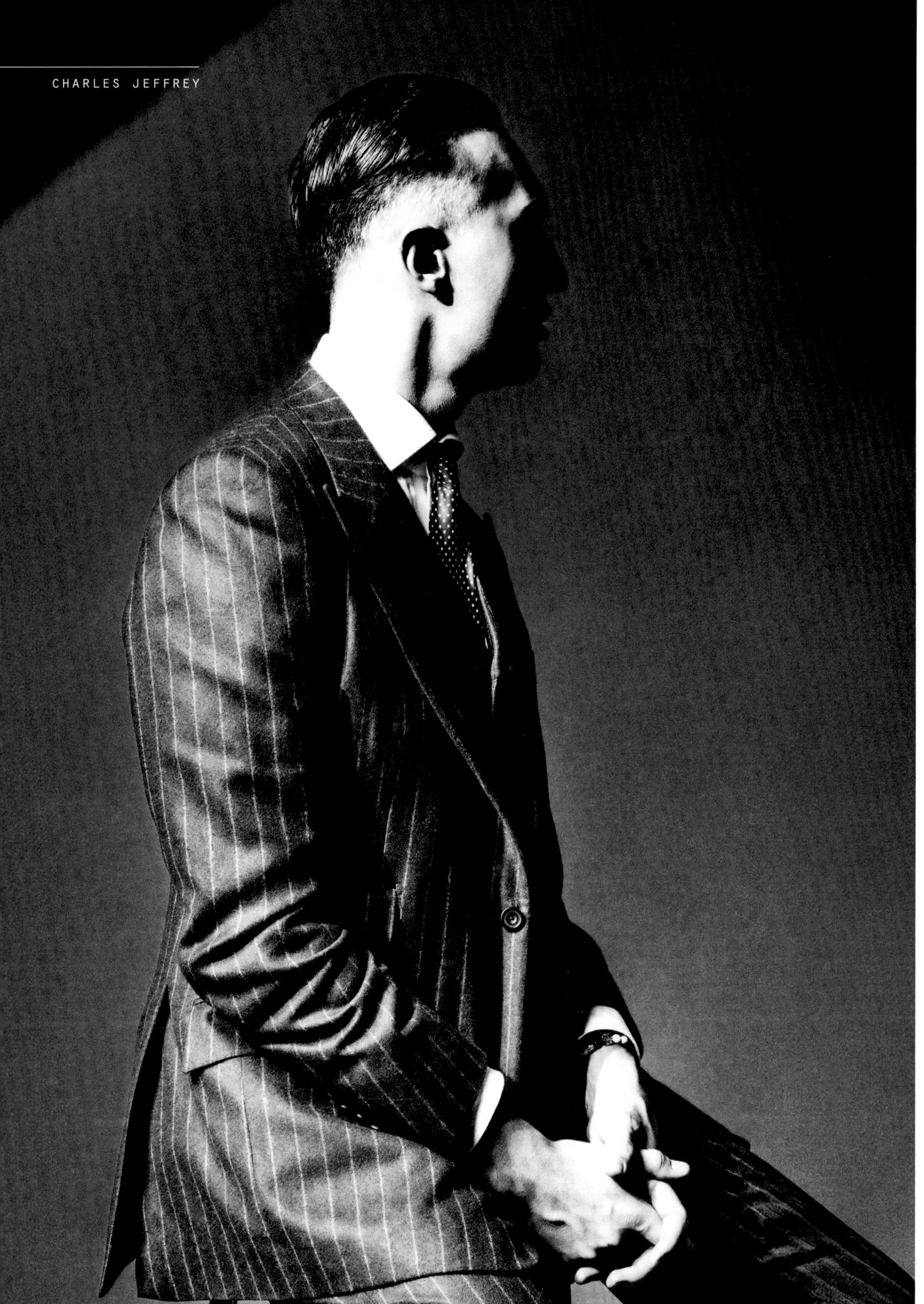

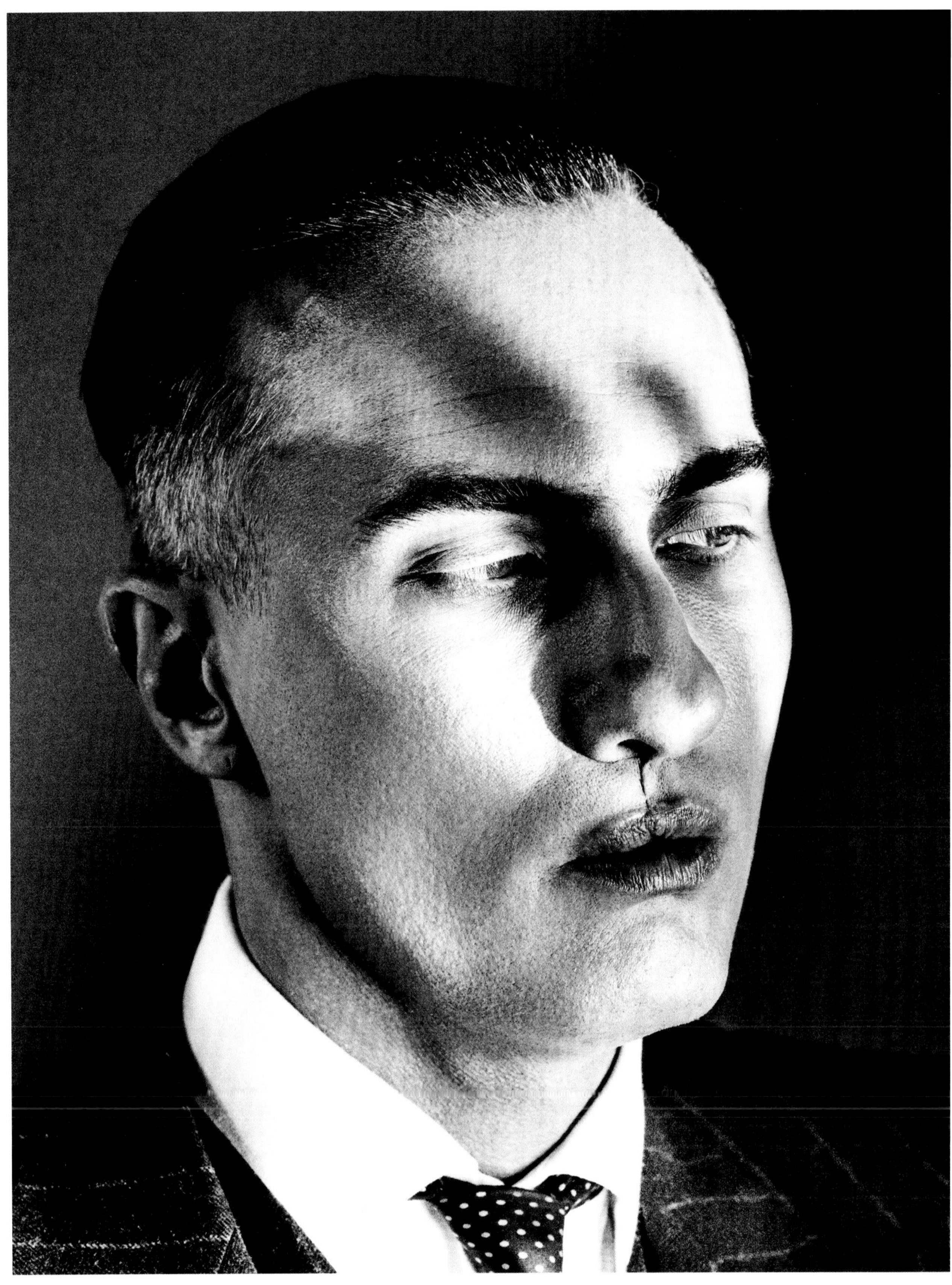

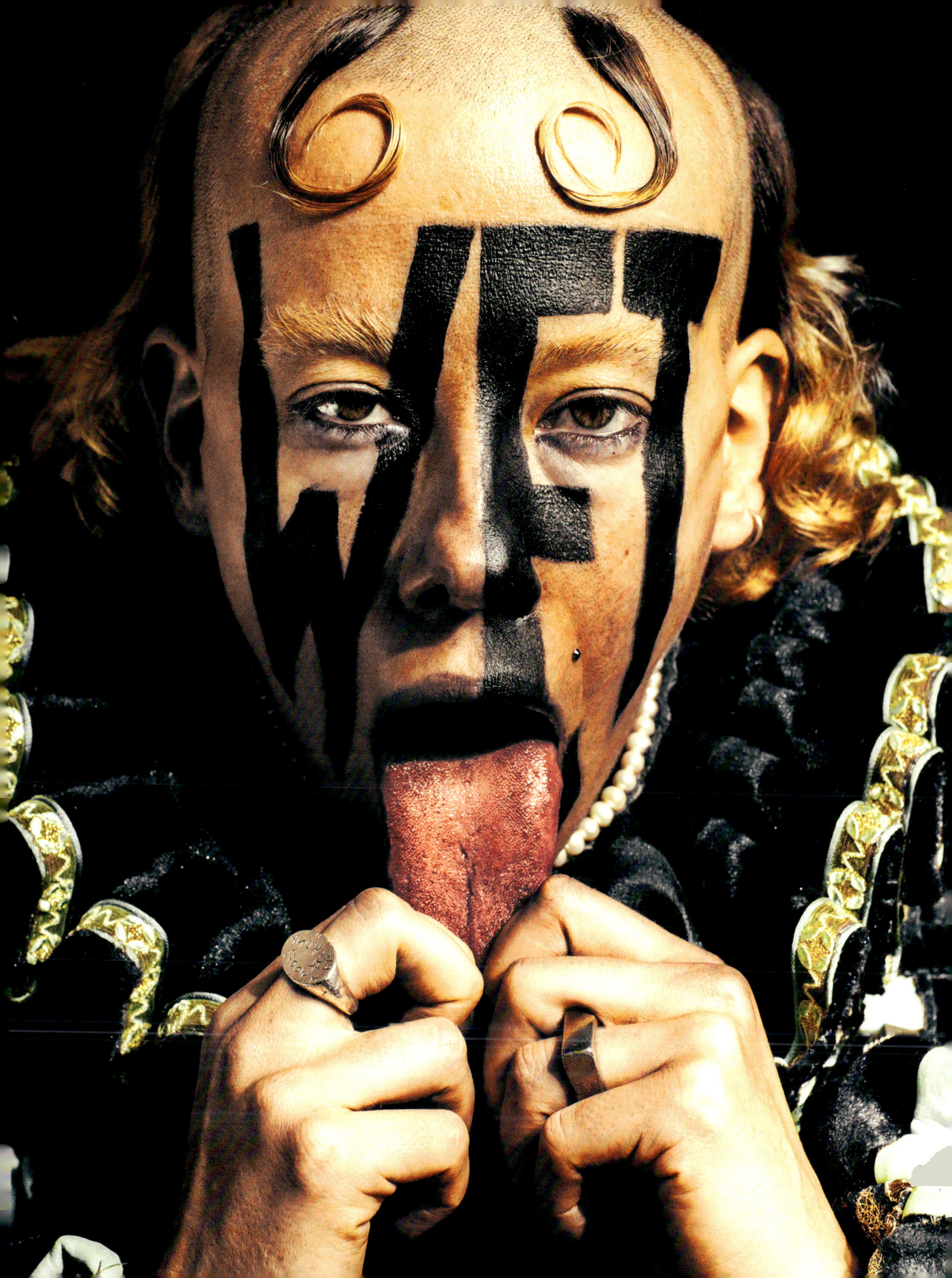
WET

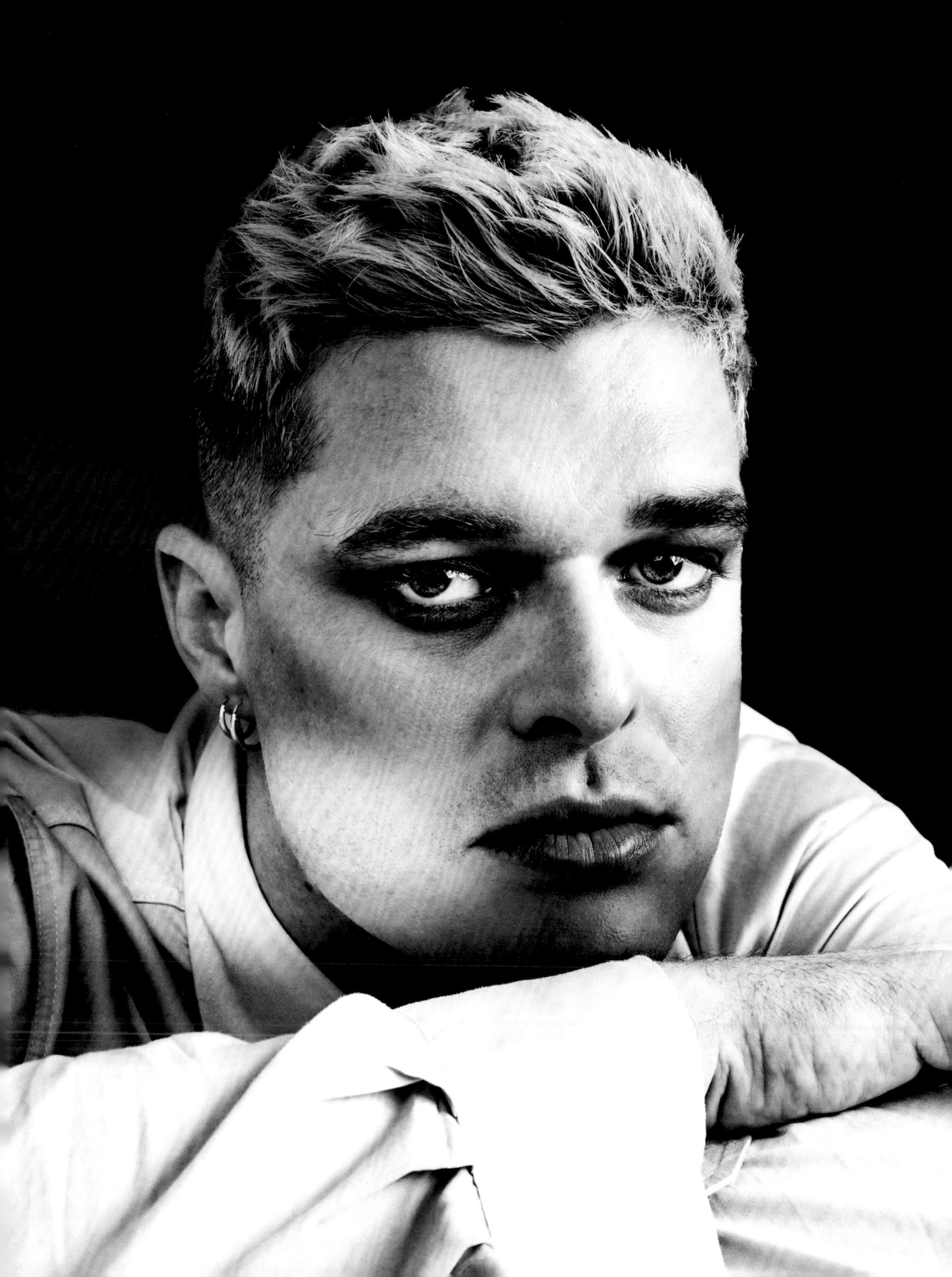

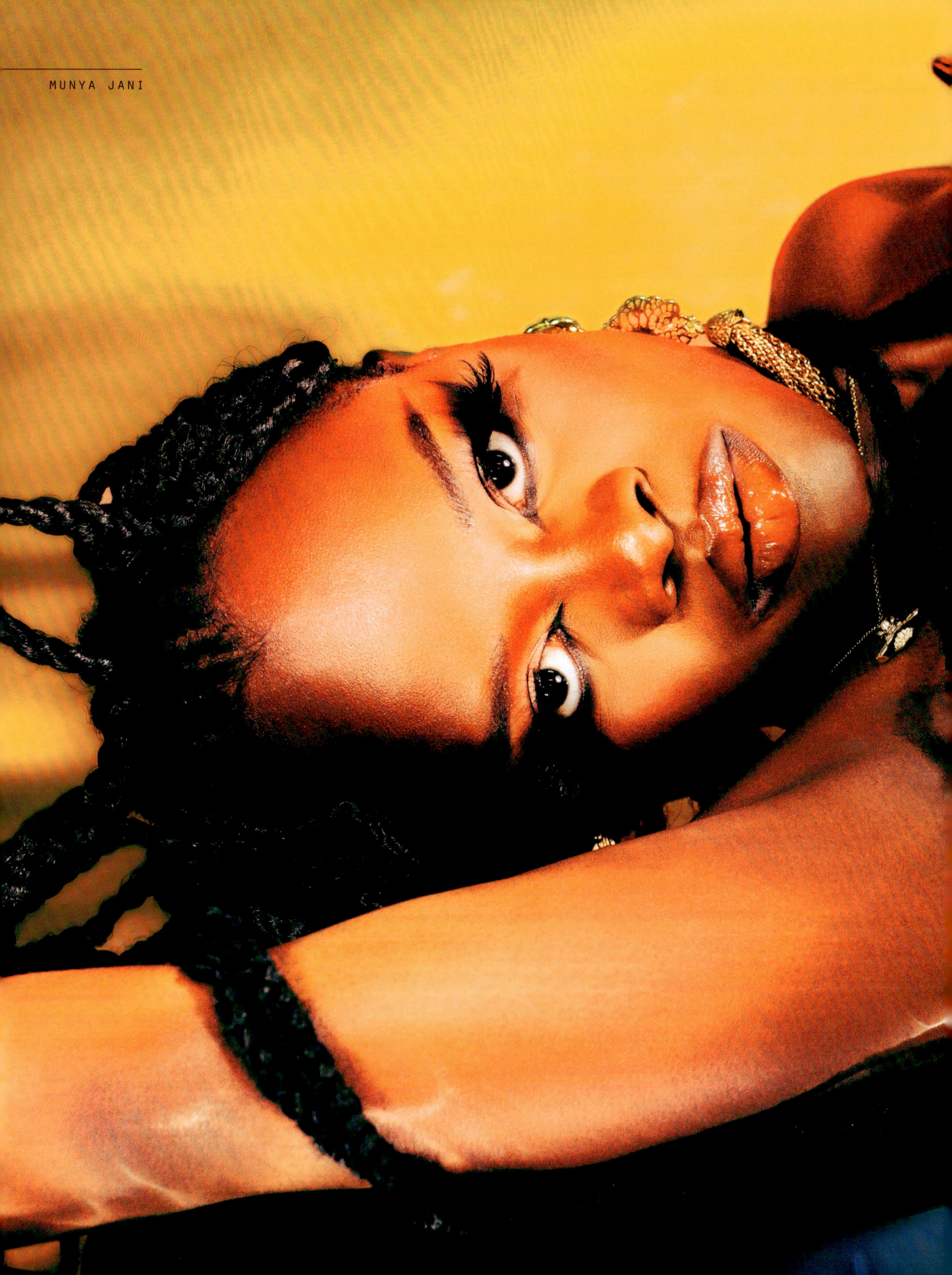
MUNYA JANI

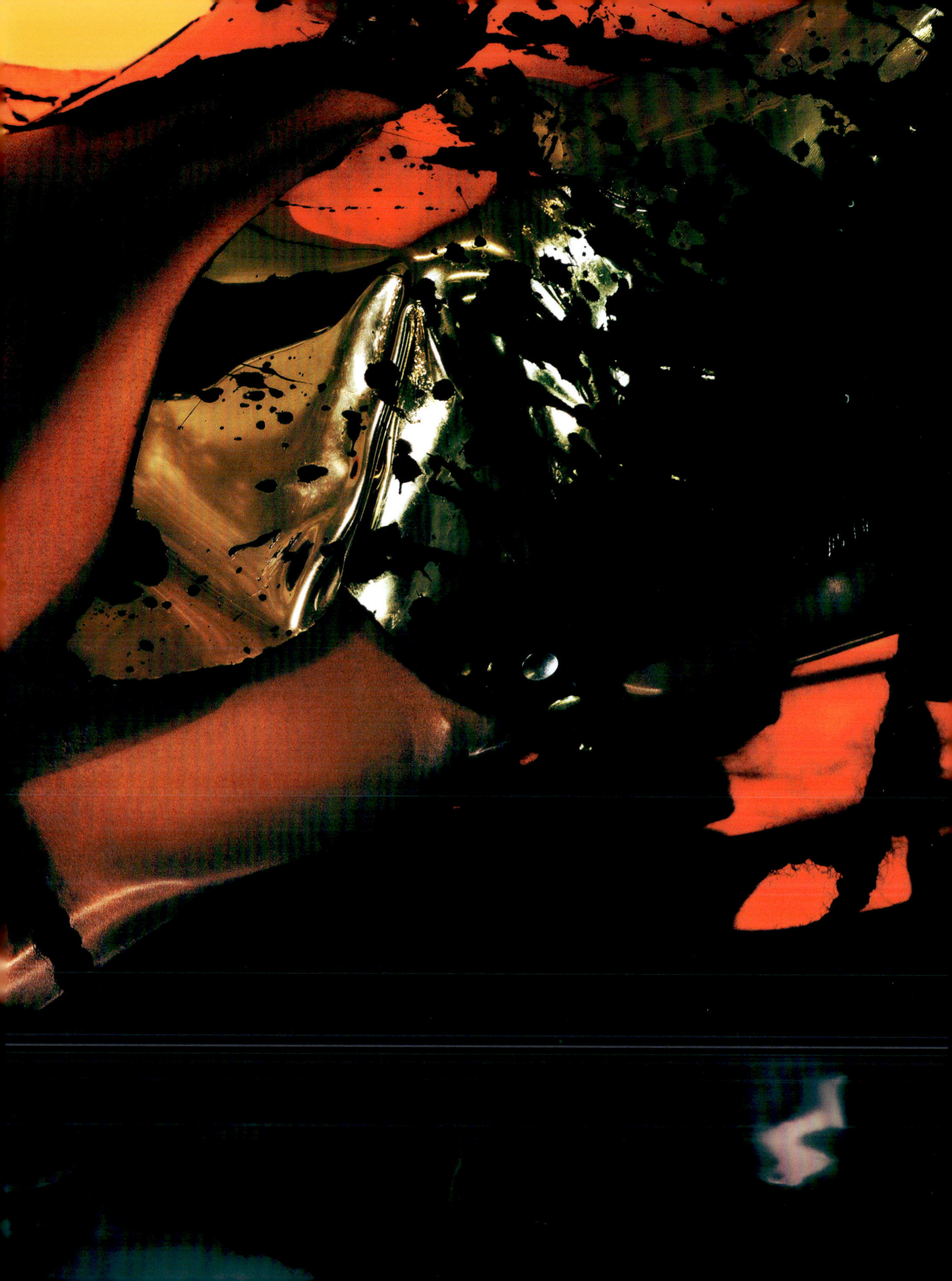

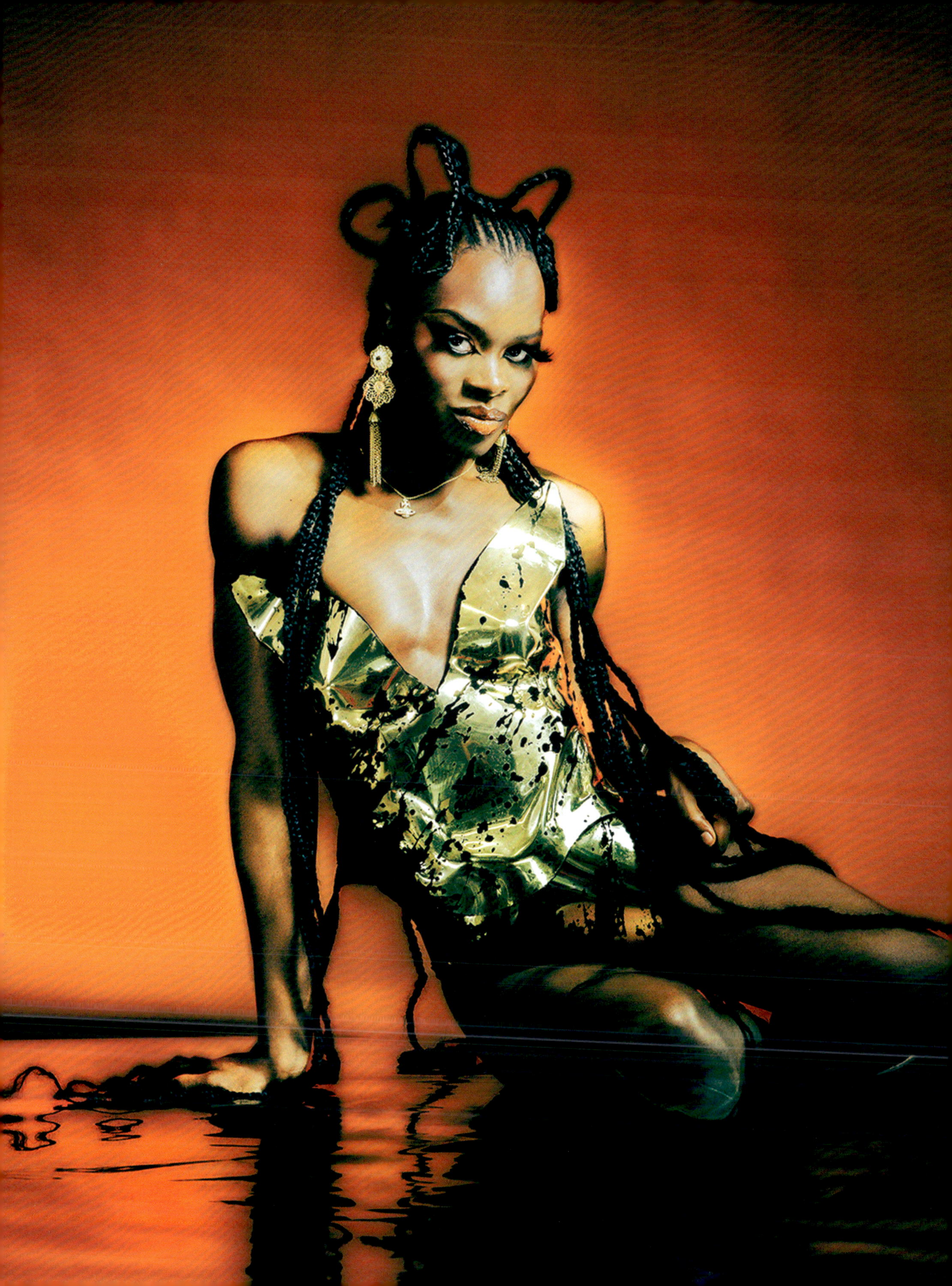

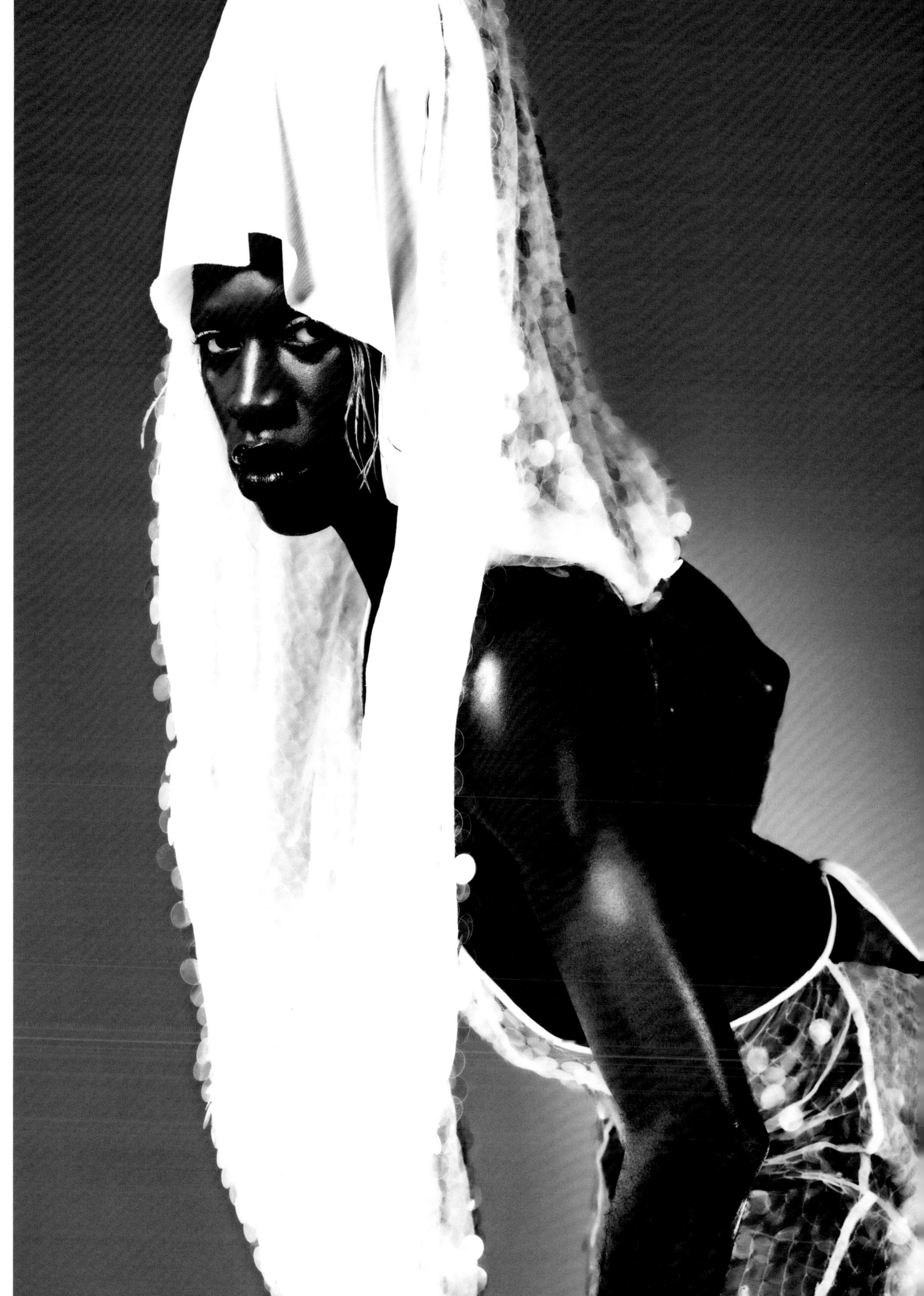

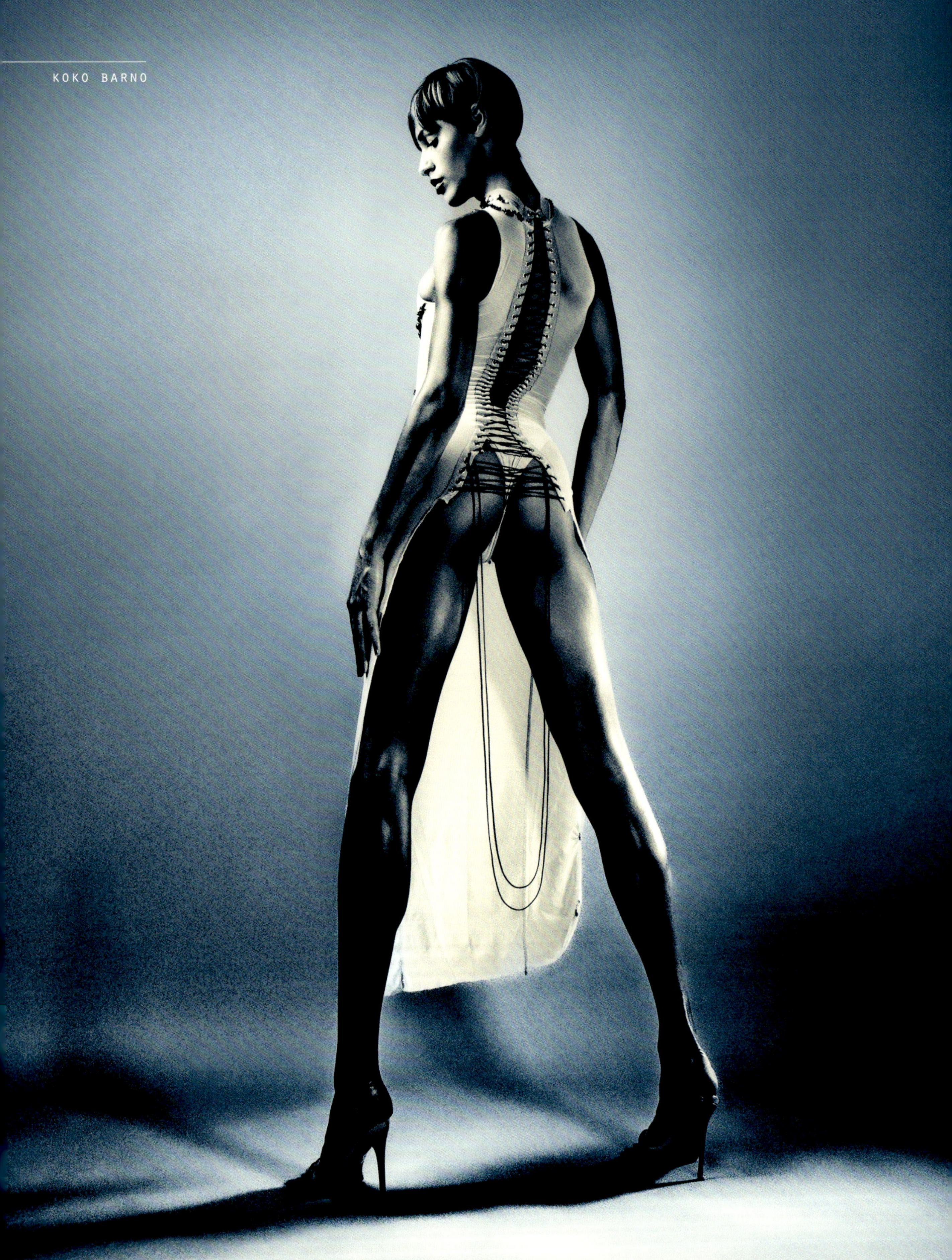

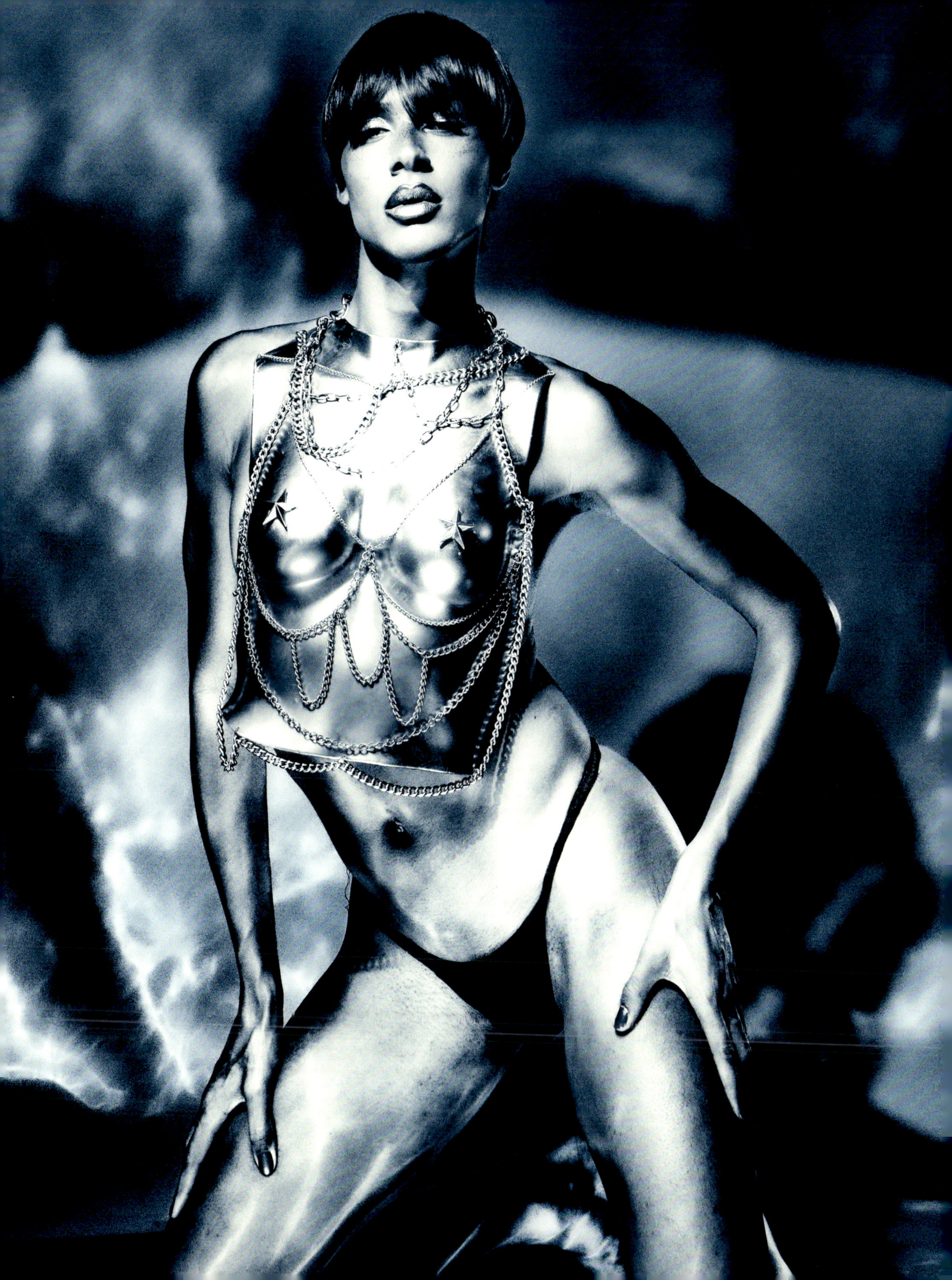

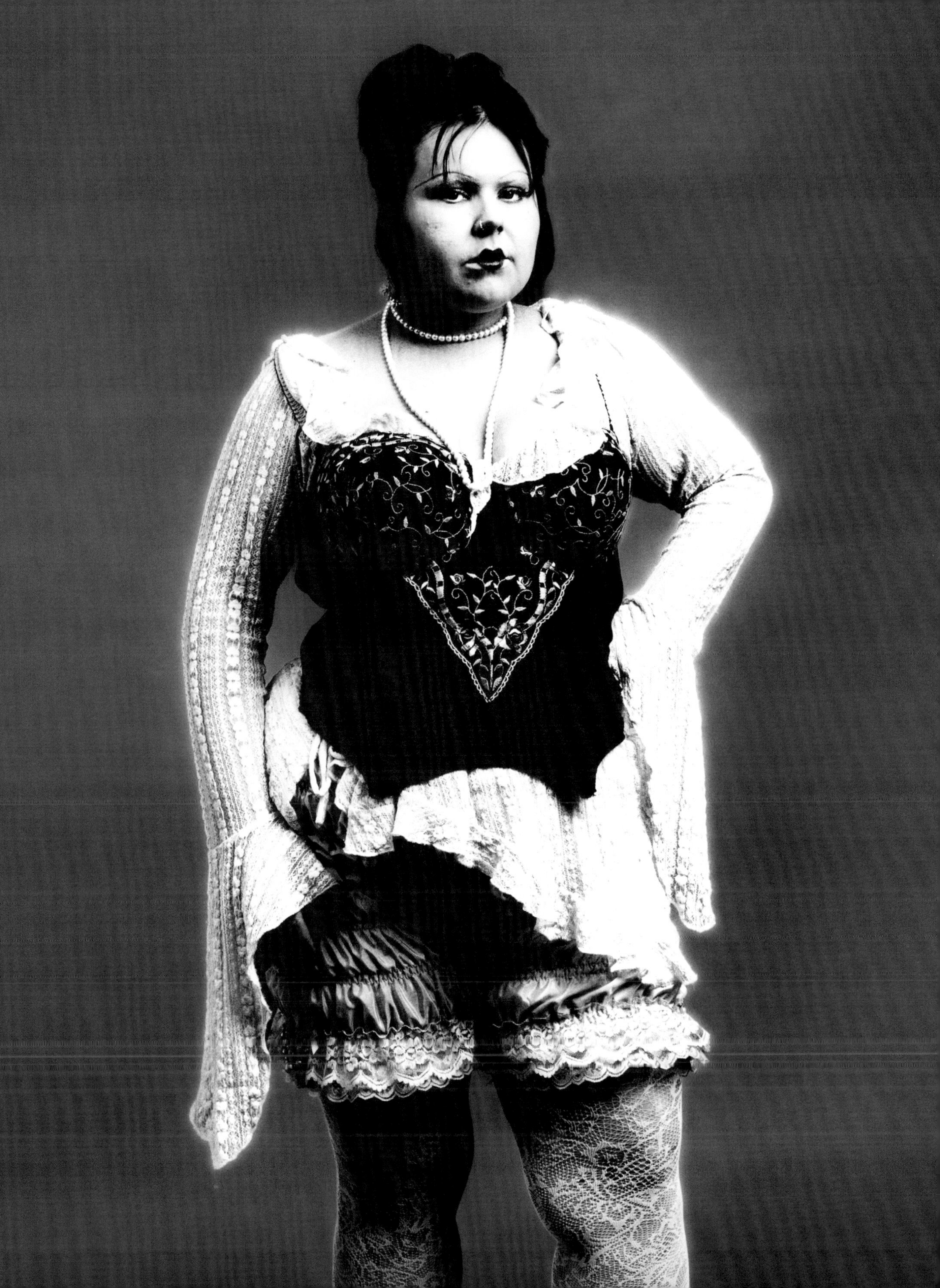

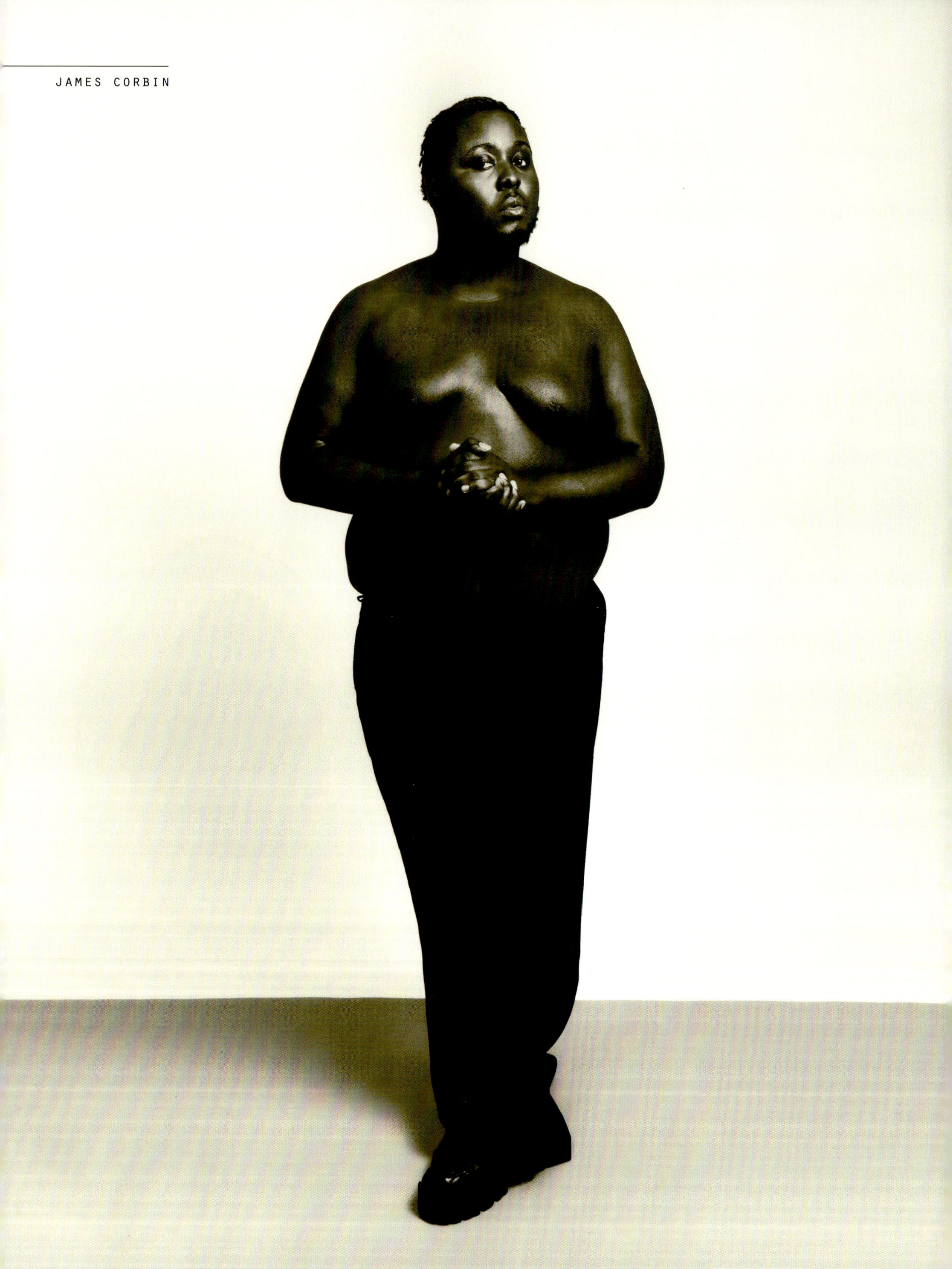
JAMES CORBIN

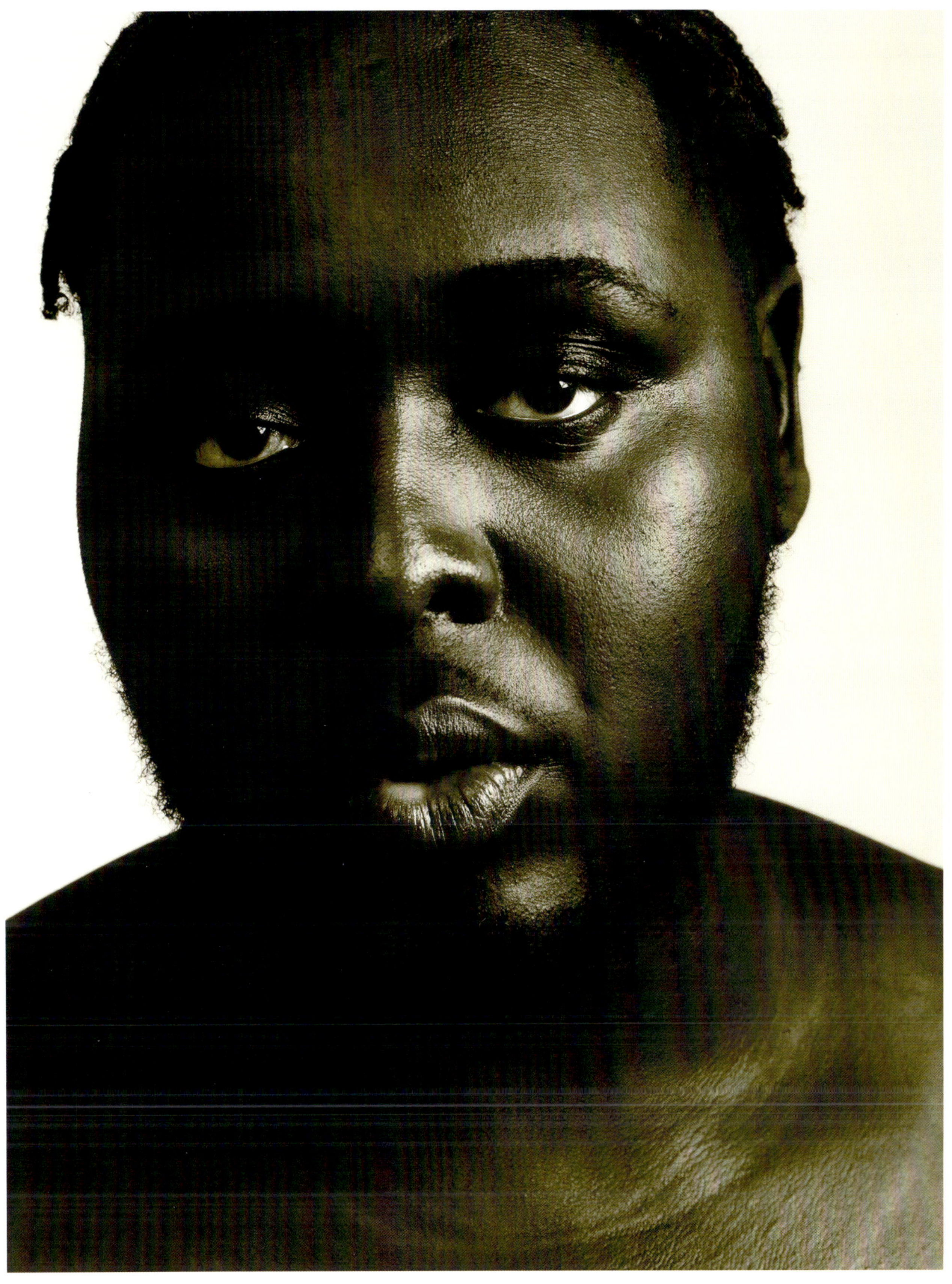

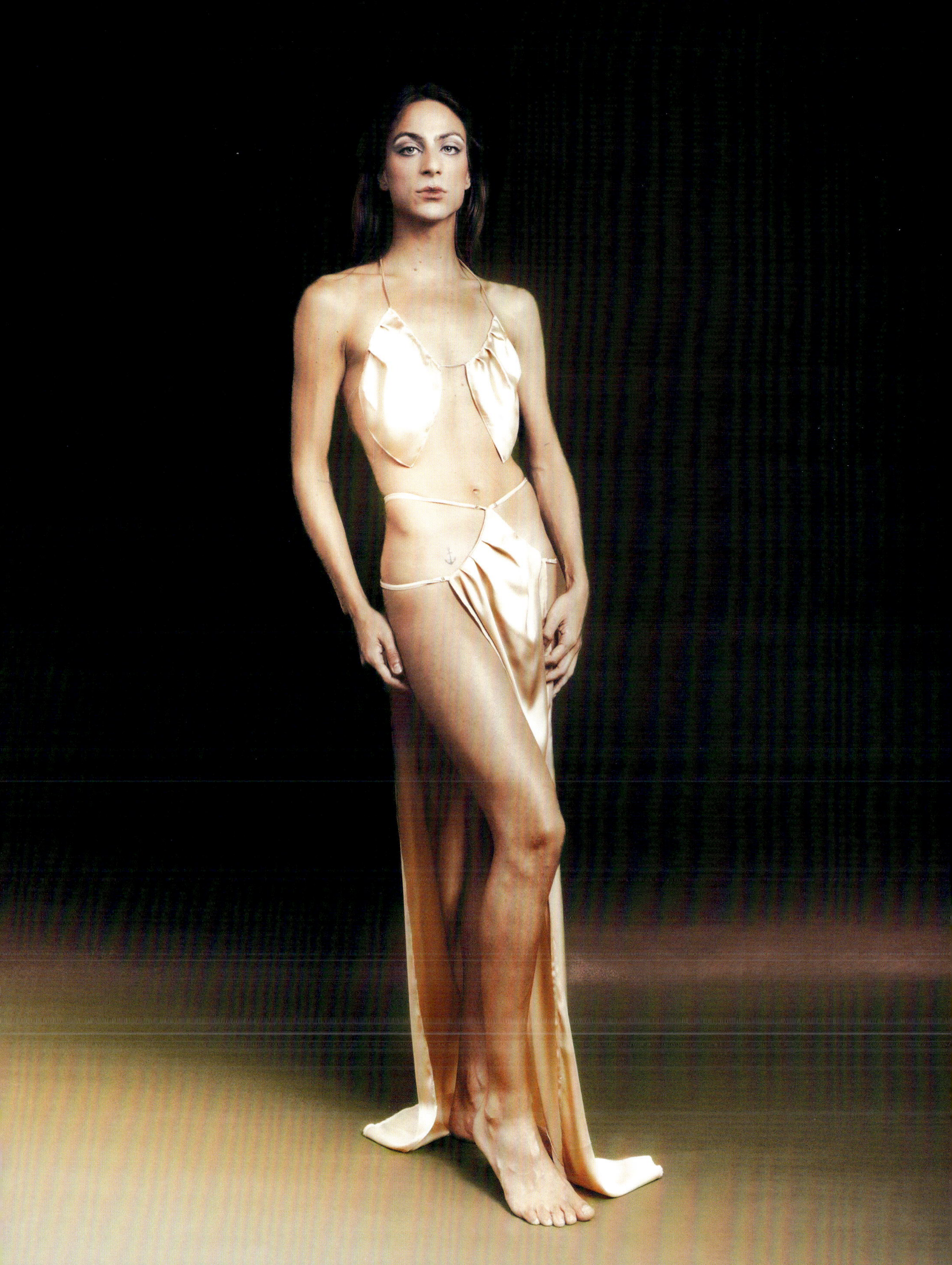

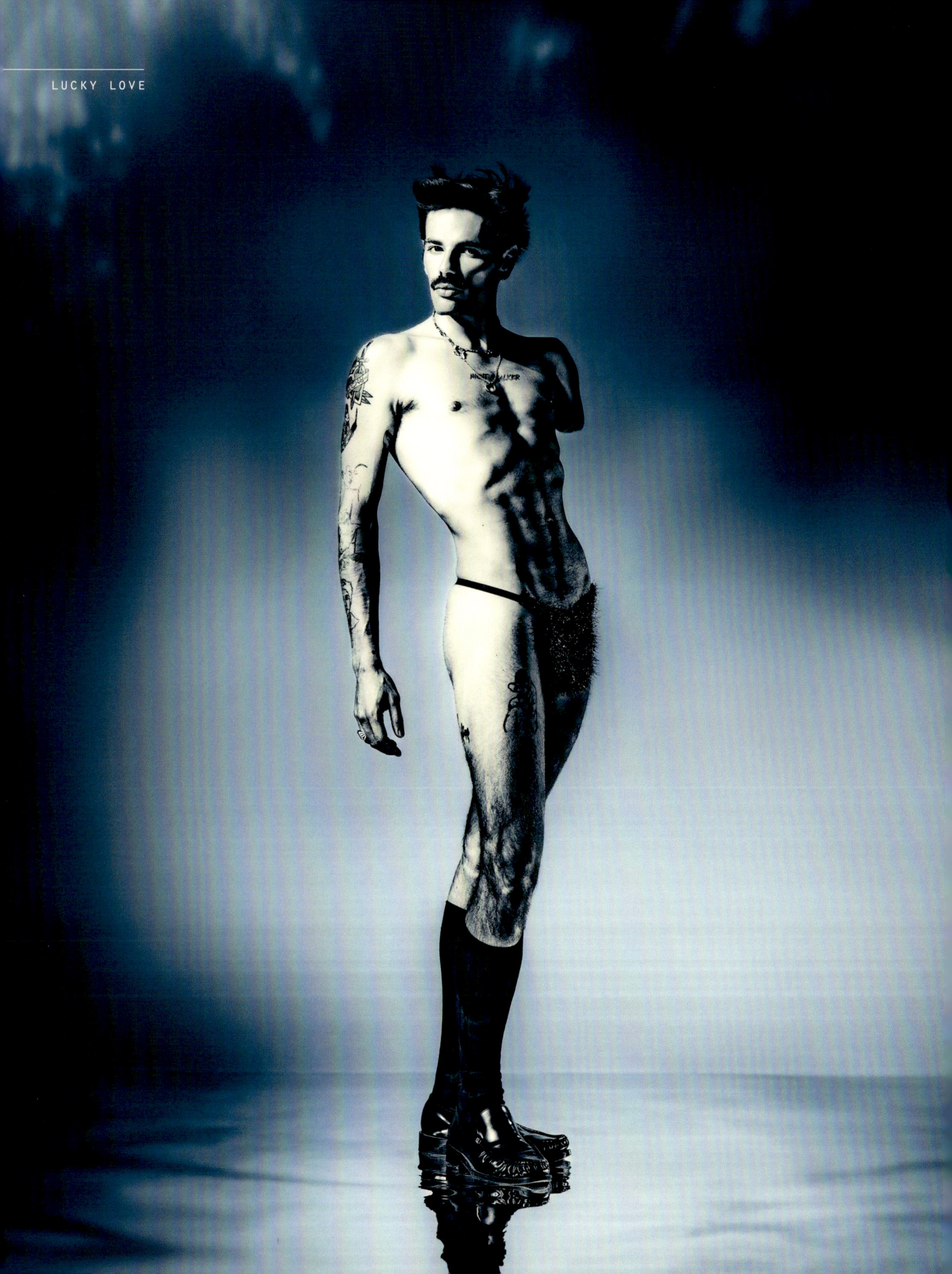

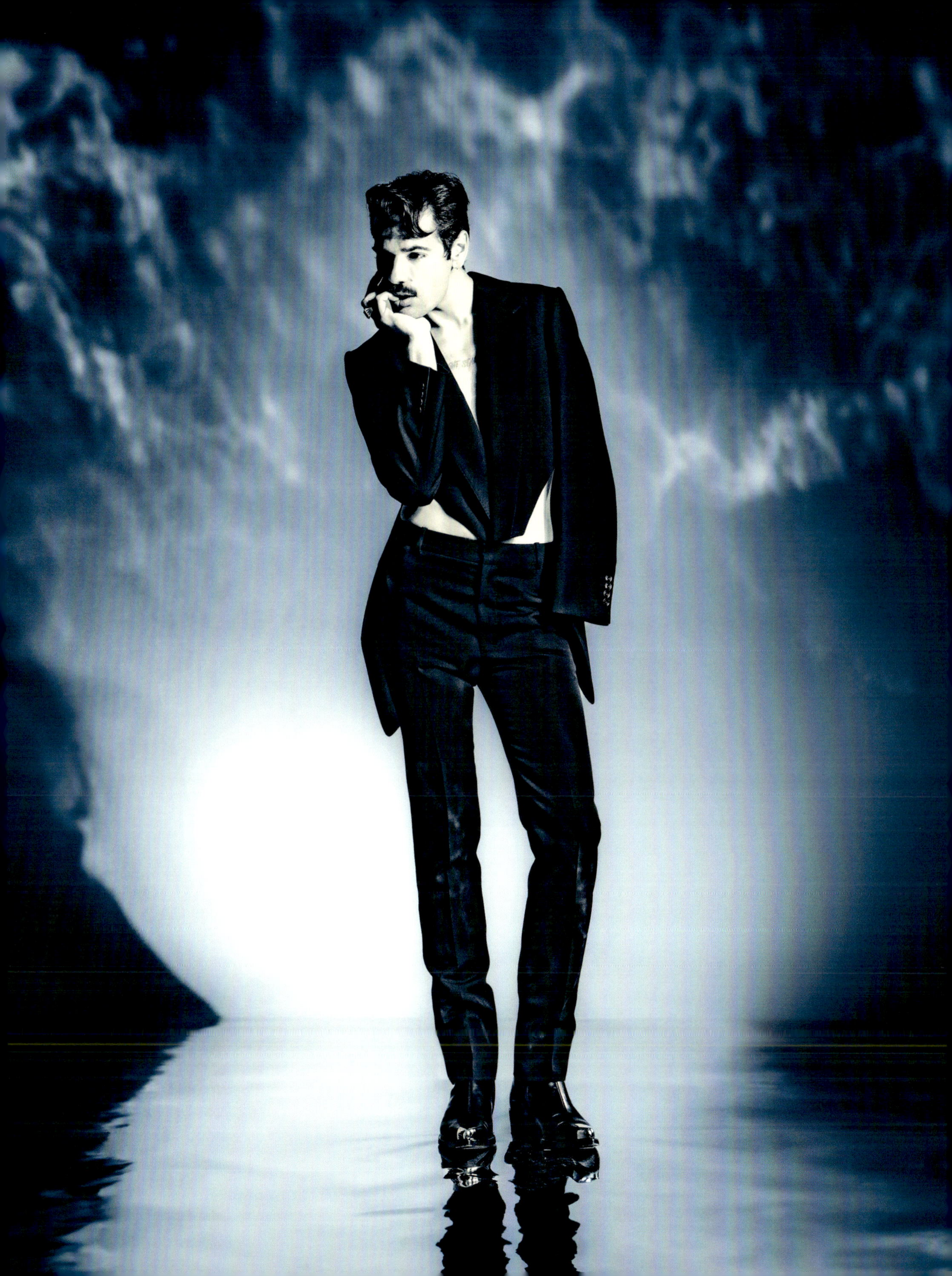

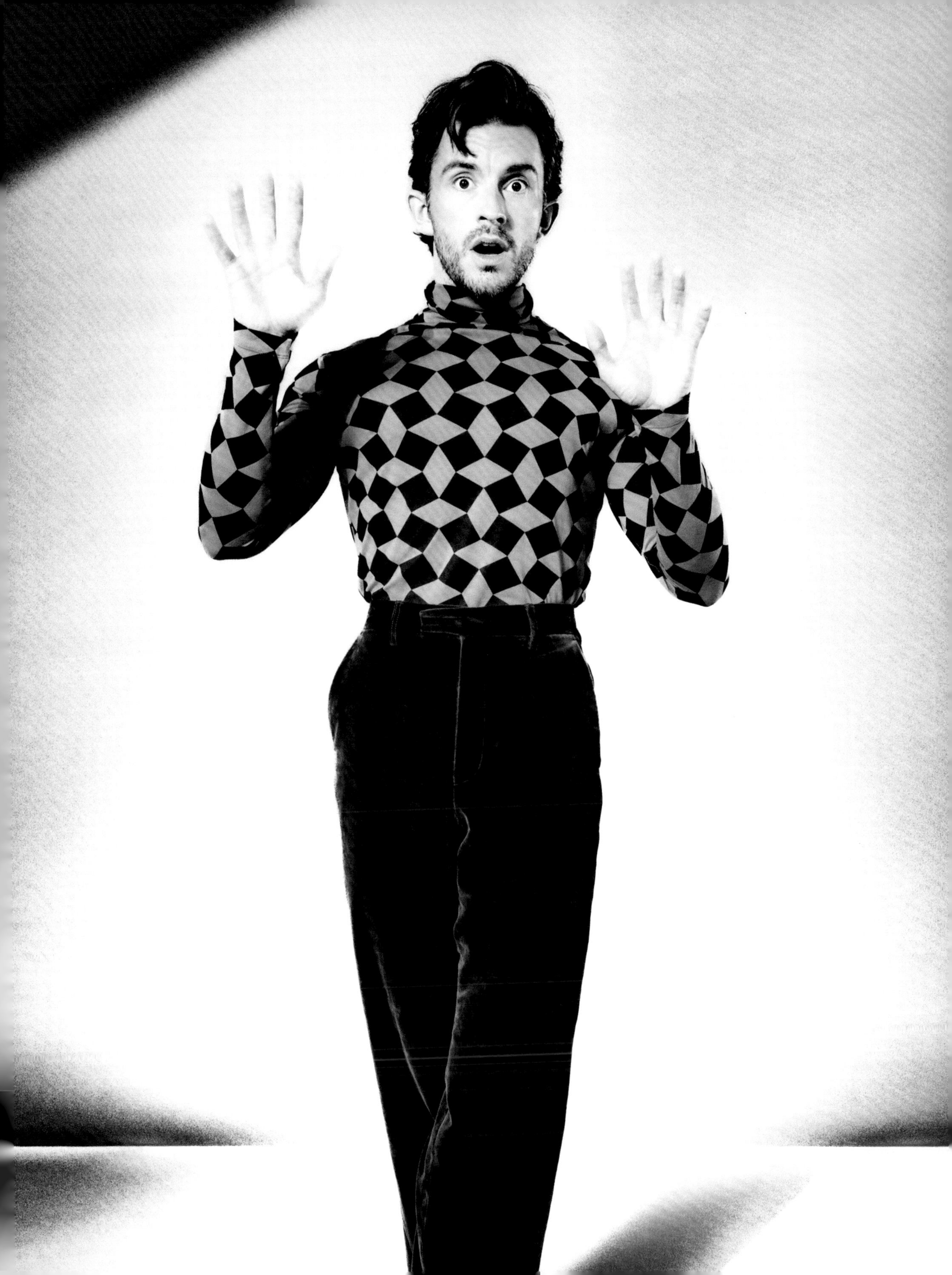

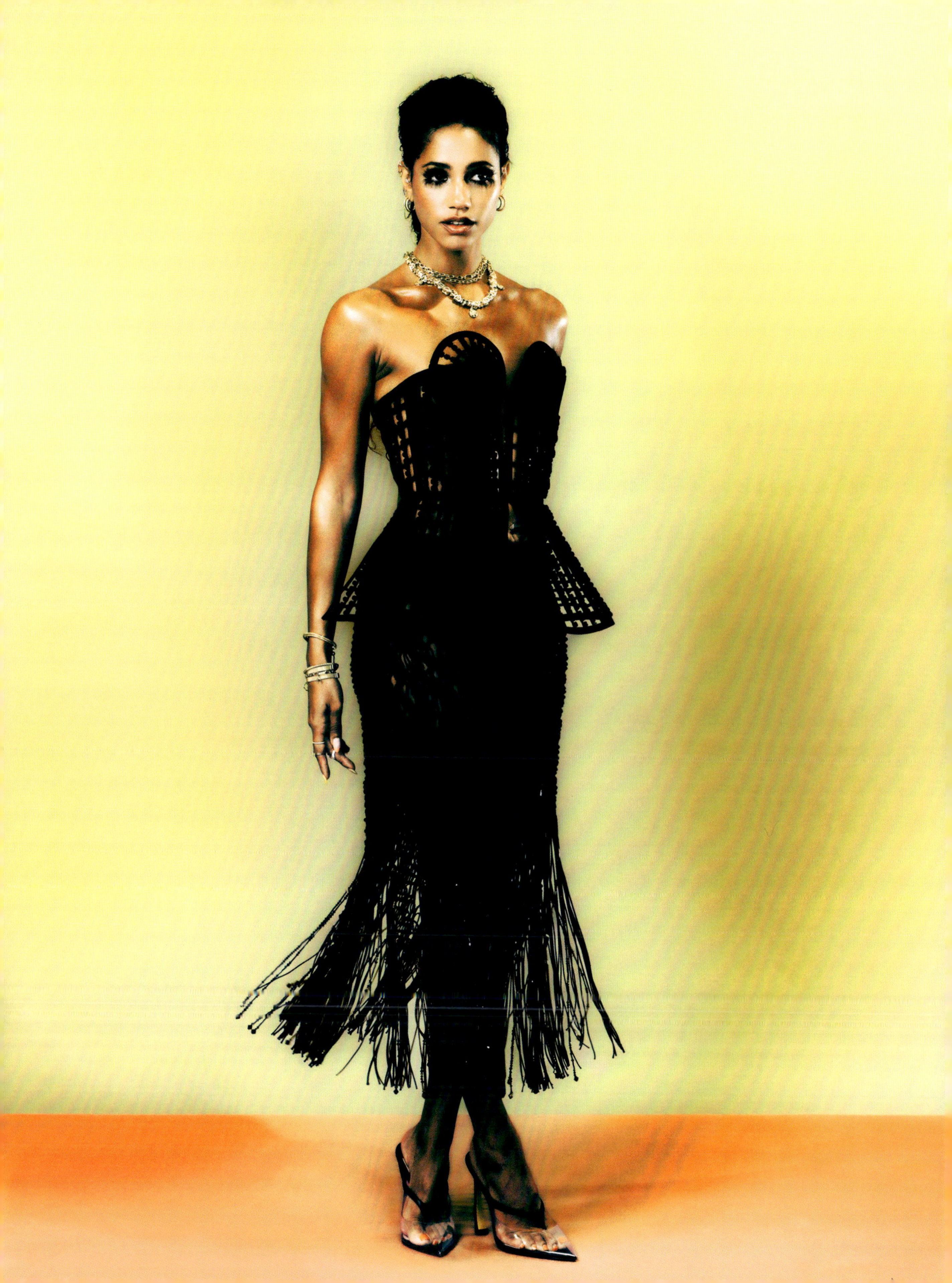

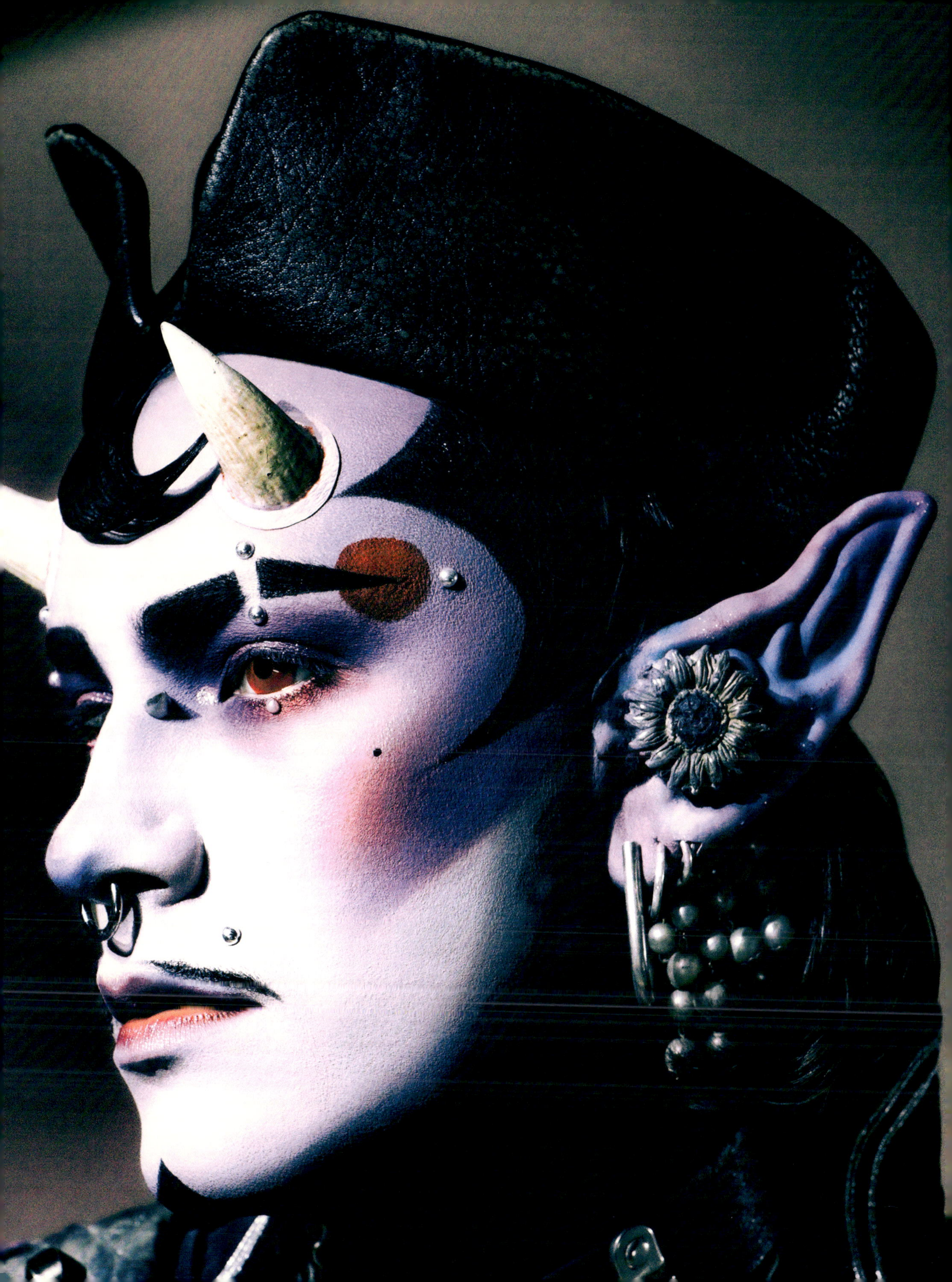

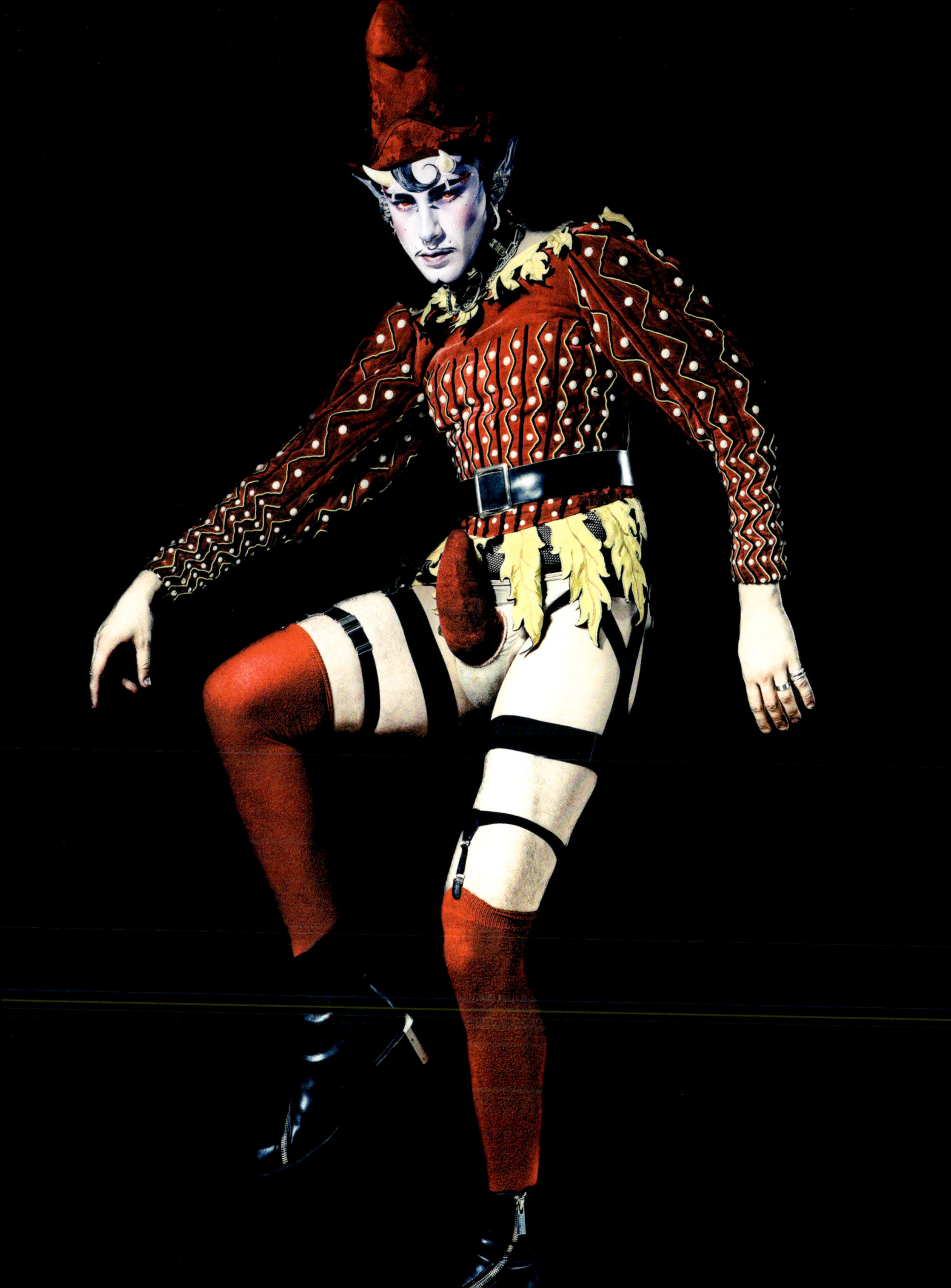

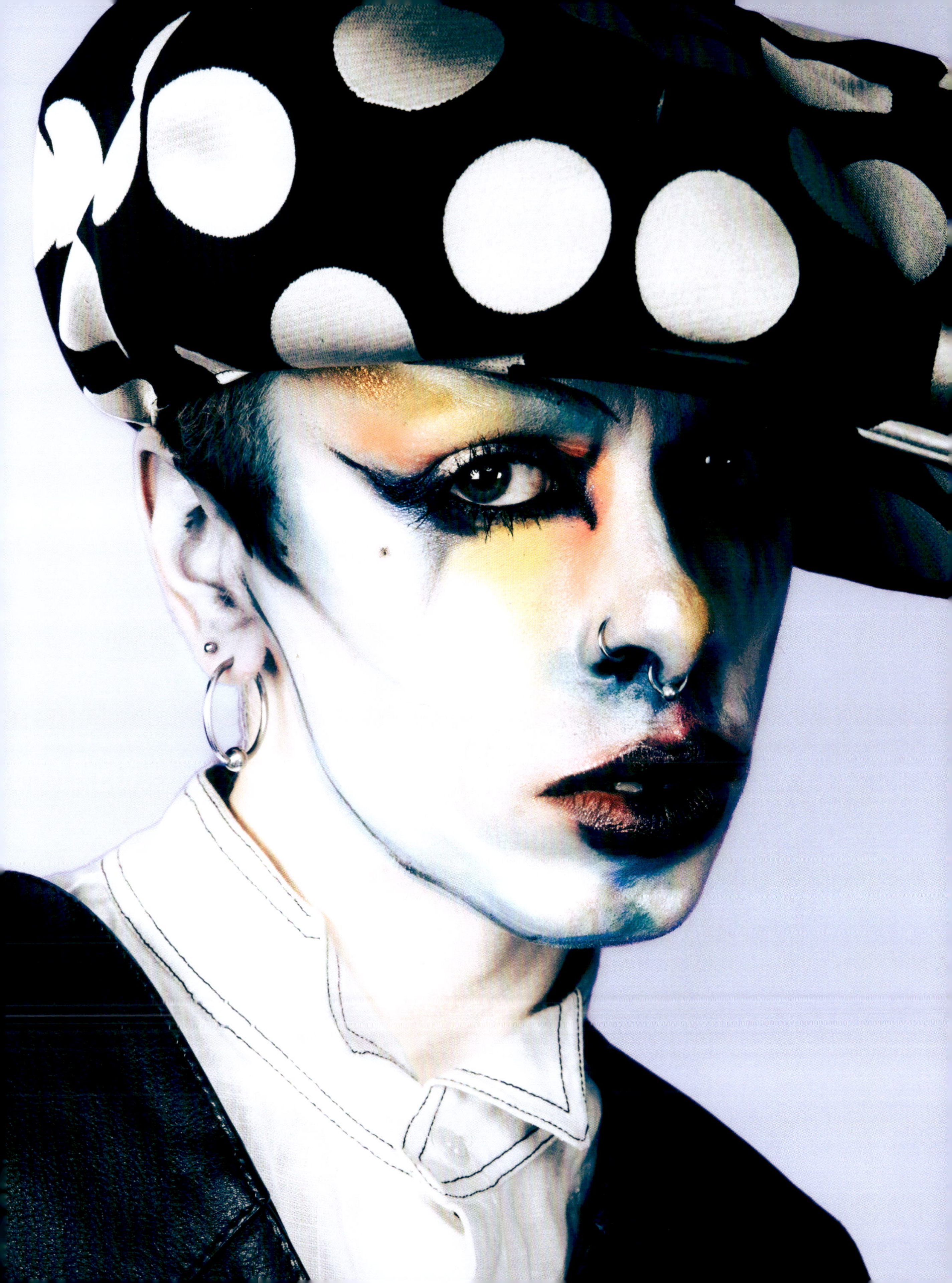

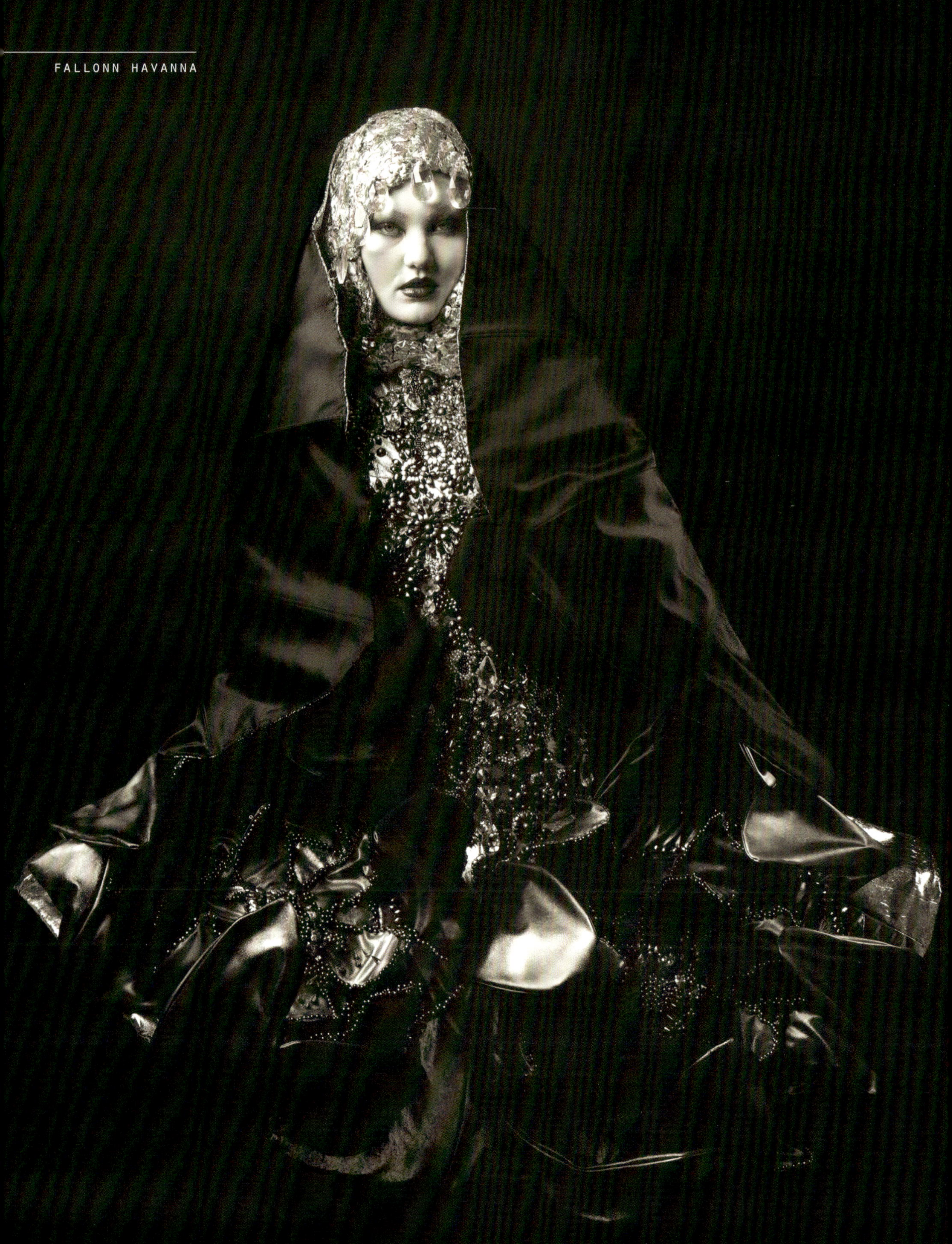

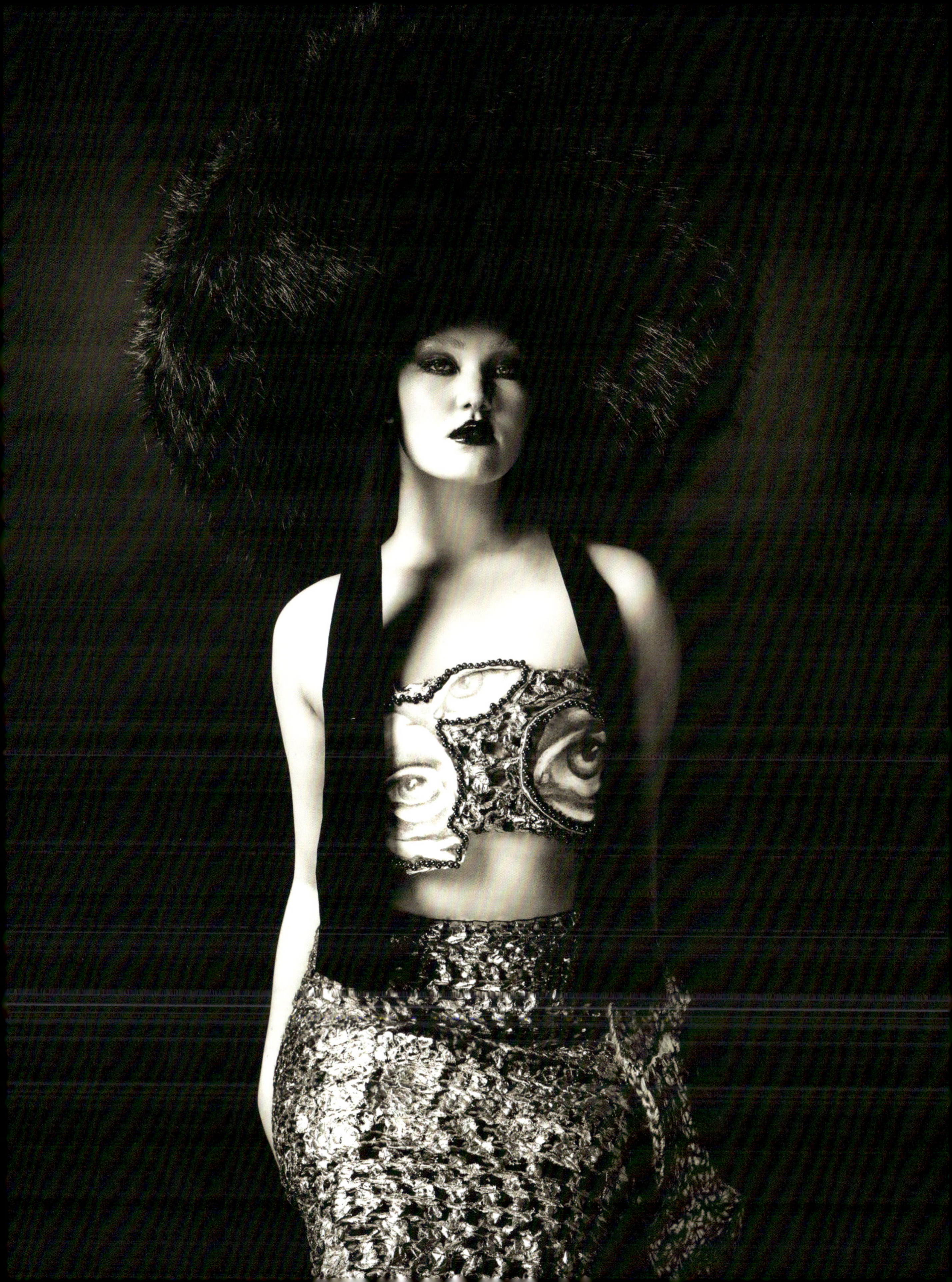

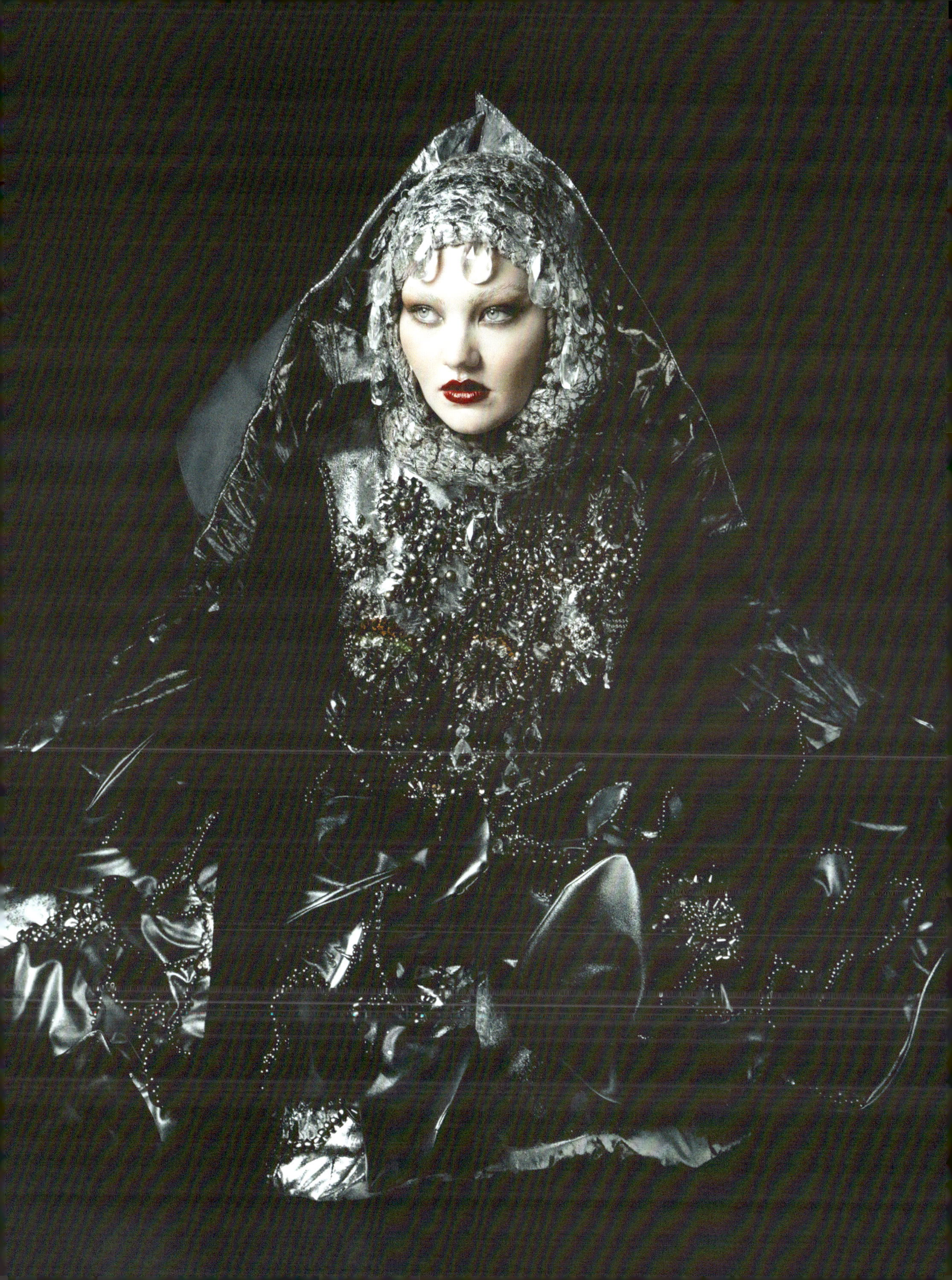

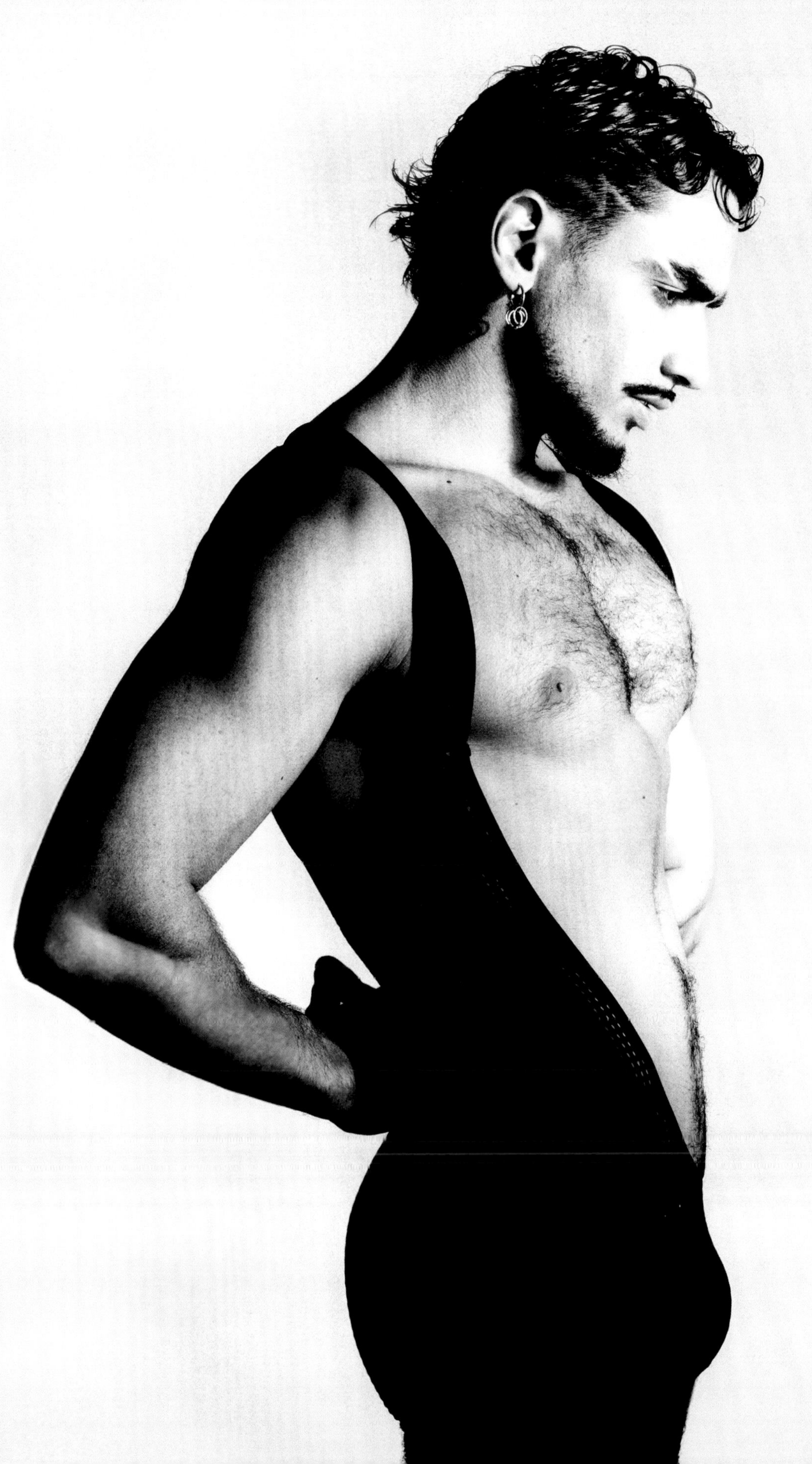

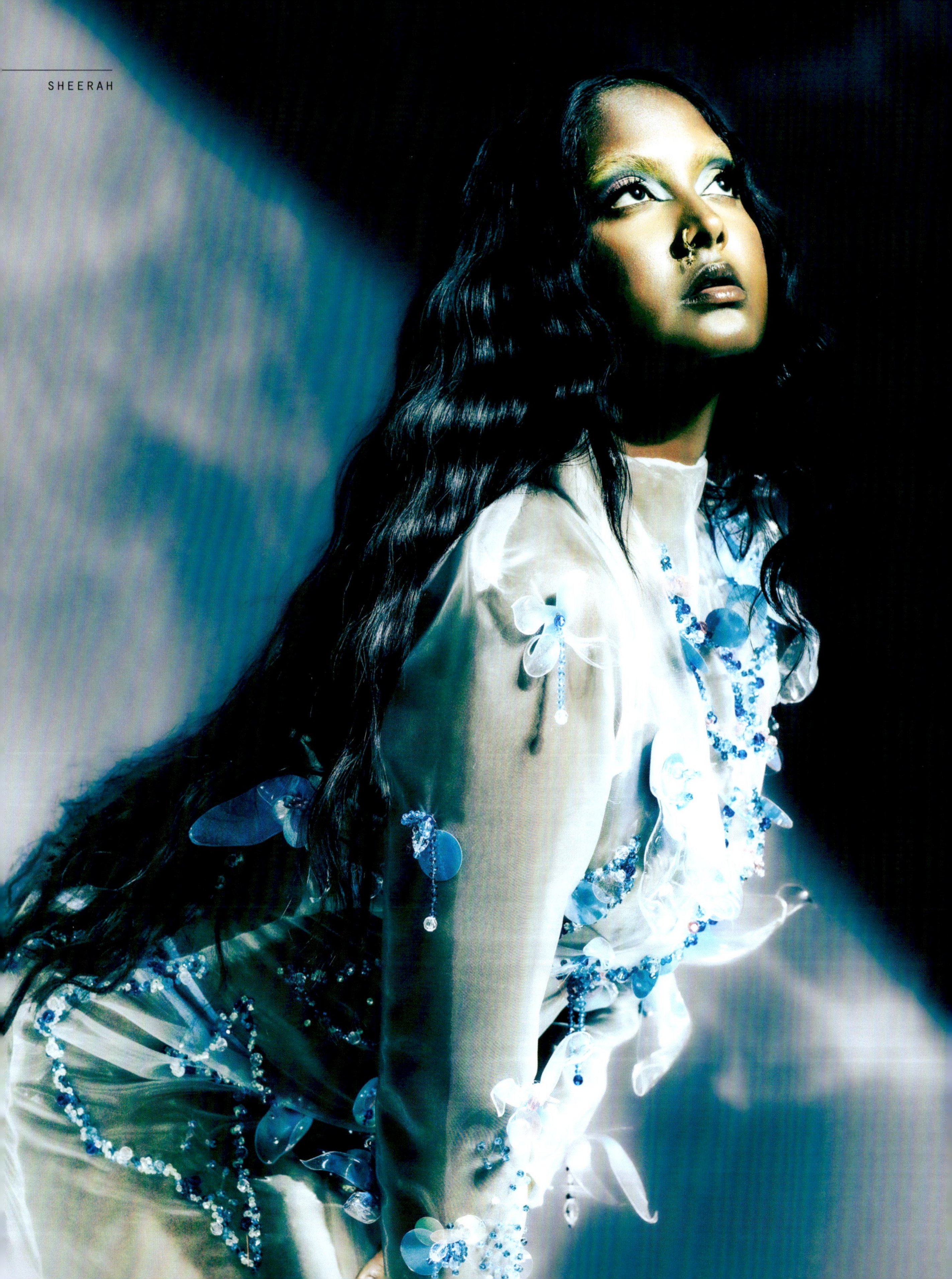

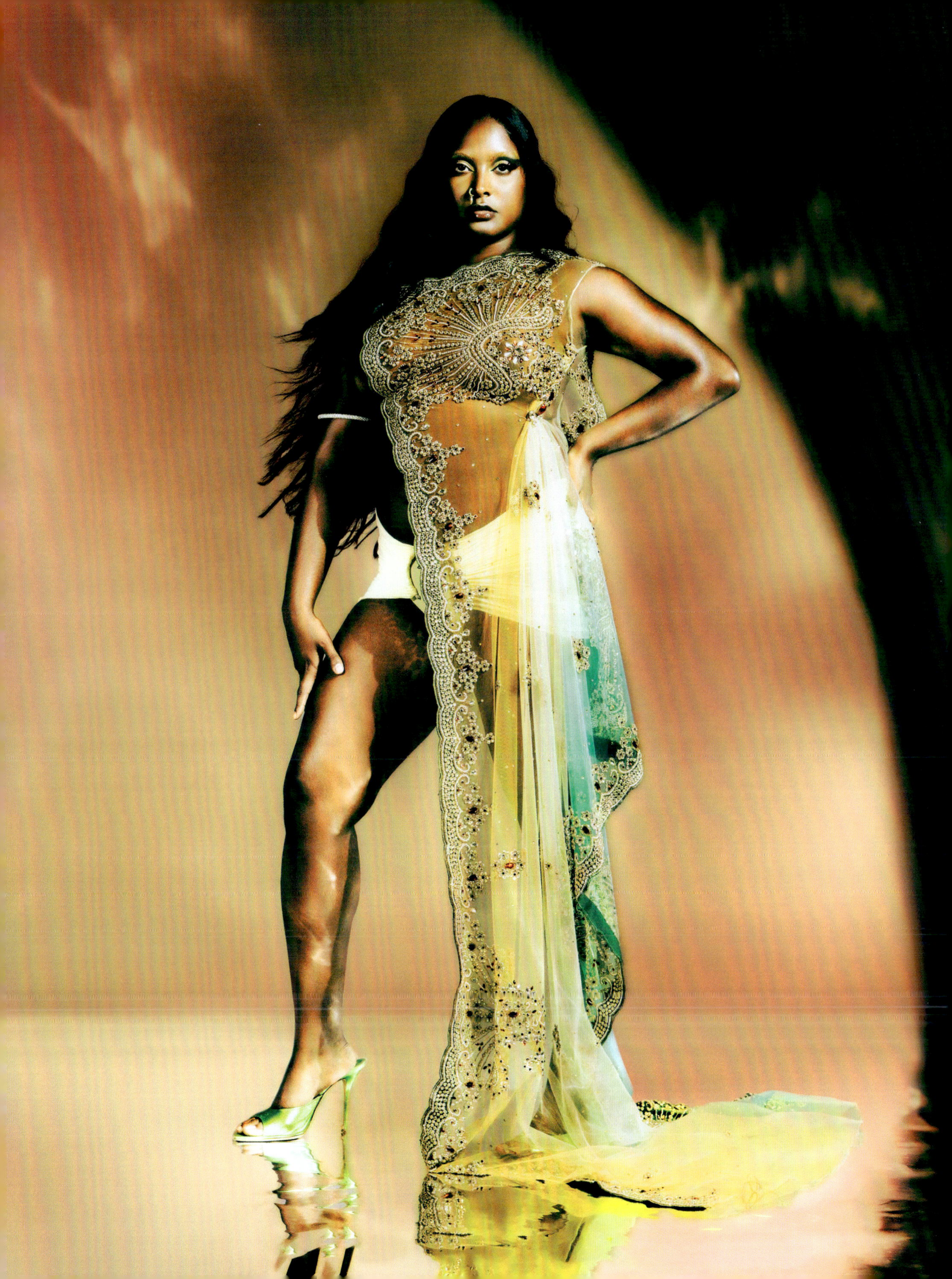

Acknowledgments

The photographs presented in this book were made possible by Jon Stryker: philanthropist, architect, and photography devotee.

This book was made possible in part by a grant from the arcus* FOUNDATION.

My heart is filled with gratitude for all the support and love I have received from everyone who has collaborated with me to create this book. A special thank you to all the individuals I have had the privilege of photographing. I am deeply thankful to everyone who supported me throughout this journey.

I especially want to express my gratitude to my mom, Daisy, for her endless patience and unconditional love. To my chosen family, Leticia Colin, Alex Galaz, Paula Turmina, and James Adams, thank you for your unwavering support and encouragement.

Thanks also to Jurek Wajdowicz for his guiding hand and inspiring advice, and the rest of the team at Emerson, Wajdowicz Studios (EWS) and The New Press for bringing this project to life. My thanks to Prishita Maheshwari-Aplin for their eloquent introduction. Finally, I am grateful for the support of Jon Stryker and the Arcus Foundation in providing a creative space for the LGBTQIA+ community.

This achievement wouldn't have been possible without all of you.
Thank you from the bottom of my heart.

—Asafe Ghalib

---

*The Arcus Foundation is a global foundation dedicated to the idea that people can live in harmony with one another and the natural world. Arcus works to advance respect for diversity among peoples and in nature (www.ArcusFoundation.org).